Paul's Letters to the
CORINTHIANS

THE MORNINGSTAR VISION BIBLE

by Rick Joyner

MorningStar Publications

Paul's Letters to the Corinthians, The MorningStar Vision Bible
by Rick Joyner
Copyright ©2013
Trade Size Edition

Distributed by MorningStar Publications, Inc.,
a division of MorningStar Fellowship Church
375 Star Light Drive, Fort Mill, SC 29715

www.MorningStarMinistries.org
1-800-542-0278

Cover and Layout Design: Kevin Lepp and Kandi Evans

ISBN— 978-1-60708-522-5; 1-60708-522-4

For a free catalog of MorningStar Resources, please call 1-800-542-0278

Paul's Letters to the Corinthians
TABLE OF CONTENTS

PREFACE
THE MORNINGSTAR VISION BIBLE
BY RICK JOYNER

Next to His Son and the Holy Spirit, The Bible is God's greatest gift to mankind. What treasure on earth could be compared to one Word from God? There is good reason why The Bible is the bestselling book of all-time by such a wide margin. The importance of The Bible cannot be overstated. If Jesus, who is the Word, would take His stand on the written Word when challenged by the devil, how much more must we be established on that Word to take our stand and live our lives by it?

The most basic purpose of **The MorningStar Vision Bible** is accuracy and faithfulness to the intended meaning of the Author, the Holy Spirit. His written Word reveals the path to life, salvation, transformation, deliverance, and healing for every soul who would seek to know God. The universe is upheld by the Word of His power, so there is no stronger foundation that we could ever build our lives on other than His Word. Therefore, we have pursued this project with the utmost care in that what is presented here is His Word and not ours. We were very careful not to let anyone work on it that had an agenda other than a love for the truth and the deepest respect for the fact that we were handling this most precious treasure—God's own Word.

The primary accuracy of any translation is its adherence to the original text in the original languages The Bible was written in, Hebrew and Greek. However, there are problems when you try to translate from a language such as Greek into a language like English because Greek is so much more expressive than English. For example, there are several different Greek words with different meanings that are translated as one word "love" in our English version. The Greek words distinguish between such things as friendship love, erotic attraction, or unconditional love. When we just translate these as "love," then it may be generally true, but something basic in what the Author tried to convey is left out. As we mature in Christ by following the Spirit, these deeper, more specific meanings become important. Therefore, we have sought to include the nuances of the Greek language in this version.

A basic biblical guide we used for this work was Psalm 12:6: **"The words of the LORD are pure words; as silver tried in a furnace on the earth, refined seven times."** Every book we release of this version has been through a meticulous process to ensure faithfulness to the original intent at least seven times. Even so, we do not consider this yet to be a completed work. We are releasing these book by book in softcover to seek even further examination by those who read it. We are asking our readers to send us challenges for any word, phrase, or part that you think may not be accurate, along with your reasons. These will be received, considered, and researched with openness. If you have insights that you think should be added to the commentary, we will consider those as well.

You can email these or any comments that you have to bible@morningstarministries.org, or mail them to us at:

MorningStar Publications
375 Star Light Drive
Fort Mill, South Carolina 29715

Please include any credentials that you might have that would be relevant, but they are not necessary for this.

My personal credentials for compiling and editing such a work are first my love for The Bible and my respect for its integrity. I have been a Christian for more than forty years, and I have read The Bible through from cover-to-cover at least once a year. I do have an earned doctorate in theology from a good, accredited school, but have not used the title because I want my message received on the merits of its content, not by a title. Though I have been in pursuit of knowing the Lord and His Word for more than forty years, I still feel more comfortable thinking of myself as a student rather than an expert. If that bothers you I understand, but when handling the greatest truth the world has ever known, I feel we must be as humble and transparent as possible.

Most of those who have worked on this project with me have been students at MorningStar University. This is a unique school that has had students from ages sixteen to over eighty years old. Some have been remarkably skilled in languages, especially Hebrew and Greek. Some have been believers and students of the Word for a long time. Others were fairly new to the faith, but were strong and devoted to seeking and knowing the truth. These were the ones that I was especially interested in recruiting for this project because of the Lord's statement in Matthew 11:25:

> **At that time Jesus answered and said, "I thank You, Father, Lord of heaven and earth, that You have hidden these things from the wise and prudent and have revealed them to babes" (NKJV).**

Because **"God resists the proud, but gives grace to the humble" (see James 4:6; I Peter 5:5 NKJV)**, the humility of a relatively young believer can be more important for discerning truth than great knowledge and experience if these have caused us to become proud.

Also, as Peter stated concerning Paul's writings in II Peter 3:15-16:

> **Paul, according to the wisdom given him, wrote to you,**
>
> **as also in all his letters, speaking in them of these things, in which are some things hard to understand, which the untaught and unstable distort, as they do also the rest of the Scriptures, to their own destruction.**

So the untaught can be prone to distort the truth if they are also unstable. This is why the relatively young believers that I sought to be a part of our team were not just stable but strong in the Lord and their resolve to know the truth.

Even so, not everyone who has great knowledge and experience has become so proud that it causes God to resist them. Those who have matured and yet remained humble and teachable are some of the greatest treasures we may have in the body of Christ. Such elders are certainly worthy of great honor and should be listened to and heeded. Nowhere in Scripture are we exhorted to honor the youth, but over and over we are commanded to honor the elders.

So it seems we have a paradox—the Lord reveals His ways to babes, but elders are the ones responsible for keeping His people on the path of life walking in His ways. This is not a contradiction. As with many of the paradoxes in Scripture, the tension between the extremes is intended to help keep us on the path of life by giving us boundaries. Pride in our experience and knowledge can cause us to stray from this path, as can our lack of knowledge if it is combined with instability. The vision and exuberance of youth are needed to keep the fire of passion for the Lord and His ways burning. This is why the Lord said that the wise brought forth from their treasures things both new and old (see Matthew 13:52).

For this reason, I sought the young in the faith who are also stable and displayed a discipline and devotion to obedience to the truth. I also sought the contributions of the experienced and learned who continued to have the humility to whom God gives His grace. As far as Greek and Hebrew scholars, I was more interested in those who are technically-minded, devoted to details, and who seemed to be free of doctrinal prejudices.

This is not to give the impression that all who worked on this project went over the entire Bible. I did have some who went over the entire New Testament, but most only worked on a single Book, and sometimes just a single issue. I may not have told many of the Greek and Hebrew experts that it was for this project when I inquired about a matter with them.

I realize that this is a unique way to develop a Bible version, but as we are told in I Corinthians 13:12 we "see in part" and **"know in part."** Therefore, we all need to put what we have together with what others have if we are going to have a complete picture. This version is the result of many years of labor by many people. Having been a publisher for many years, I know every editor or proof-reader will tend to catch different things, and so it has been with this project. We also realize that as hard as we have worked on being as accurate as possible, we may have missed some things, and we will be genuinely appreciative of every one that is caught by our readers. Again, our goal is to have the most accurate English version of The Bible possible.

Even though accuracy and faithfulness to the original intent of the Holy Spirit were our most basic devotions, we also sought insights that could come from many other factors, such as the culture of the times in which the different Books of The Bible were written. Along with myself, many other contributors have spent countless hours of research examining words, phrases, the authors of the Books of The Bible, their times, and even the history of cities and places mentioned in it. Though the knowledge gained by this research did not affect the words in the text of The Bible, they sometimes gave a greater illumination and depth to their meaning that was profound. Sometimes they made obscure, hard to comprehend phrases come to life.

One of the obvious intents of the Author was to be able to communicate to any seeker of truth on the level they are on. For the most basic seeker, knowing such things as the nuances or more detailed meaning of the Greek or Hebrew words may not be important. As we mature, we will seek deeper understanding if we follow the Holy Spirit. We are told in I Corinthians 2:10, **"For to us God revealed them through the Spirit; for the Spirit searches all things, even the depths of God."** Therefore, those who follow the Spirit will not be shallow in their understanding of anything and will especially search to know the depths of the nature of God.

Our single greatest hope is that **The MorningStar Vision Bible** will reveal accurately the will and intent of the Lord, and compel all who read it to love Him more, which is the chief purpose of man. If we love Him more, we will then begin to love one another more. As we grow in love, we will also grow in our devotion to know Him even more, know His ways, and do the things that please Him. He deserves this from us more than ever could be expressed.

There is nothing greater than knowing Him. I am convinced that anything we learn about God will make us love Him more, which is our chief purpose and the one thing that will determine if we are successful human beings. This is also the only thing that can lead to the true peace and joy that is beyond anything this world could supply. There is no greater adventure that could be had in this life than the true Christian life. The Bible is the map to the greatest quest and the greatest adventure that we could ever experience.

INTRODUCTION
PAUL'S LETTERS TO THE CORINTHIANS

The Apostle Paul's two letters to the Corinthians are unique among New Testament writings. However, the issues he addresses in them have been common in Christianity throughout the Church Age. Therefore, even though they do not address crucial doctrinal issues such as law and grace, these are two of the most important letters in Christian history for addressing the most common issues and problems in Christianity.

For example, the cause of divisions in the church at Corinth can be found at the root of almost every church split, as well as the breakup of movements and the fracturing of the church into denominations.

There is a church life that is required for true spiritual maturity in Christ. This is addressed in depth in Paul's letter to the Ephesians. The Greek word used for the community of believers is *ecclesia* or congregation. This word describes the organization and governmental structure of the church.

There is another Greek word used for church life itself, which is the Greek word *koinonia*. This word is translated as both "fellowship" and "communion" in English translations. These are accurate to a degree, but superficial in conveying the depth of the meaning of this word. *Koinonia* implies a bonding together so complete that members cannot live or exist apart from one another, just as an arm or a leg cannot exist apart from the rest of the body. This *koinonia* is so crucial to the life of a believer that not having it is the only reason given in Scripture for the weakness, sickness, and premature death of believers (see I Corinthians 10 and 11).

Therefore, *ecclesia* provides the order and structure necessary for providing the place where *koinonia* can happen. Paul's letters to the Corinthians address these two aspects of what the church is called to be in a more practical way than any other New Testament writing.

These letters encompass everything from practical church life—including church discipline—to the purpose of love and the importance of sound doctrine on the resurrection of the dead. The Apostle Paul was devoted to not merely giving instructions, but also to sharing with believers "why" the instructions were important. This is in keeping with the core purpose of the gospel—to change peoples' hearts, not just their behavior. For this reason, no other writings ever penned have changed more hearts than the letters of the Apostle Paul. These two letters to the Corinthians stand as the most powerful of all.

Paul's First Letter To The
CORINTHIANS

This letter was written by the Apostle Paul to one of the important churches of the first century, the church in Corinth, Greece. He planted this church during his second missionary journey, approximately 50-51 A.D. (see Acts 18:1-18). Paul wrote this pastoral letter in response to reports about problems arising in this young church. He wrote this letter near the end of his time in Ephesus, approximately 55-56 A.D. (see I Corinthians 16:8).

It was reported that the Corinthian church was dealing with pride, division, and licentiousness in some of its members. The church was excusing sexual sin, the improper use of spiritual gifts, and the tolerance of destructive false doctrines. In response to these issues, Paul wrote like a wise parent, lovingly but sternly, correcting his child. He sought to impart not just sound doctrine moored to Scripture, but also a love for truth and the discernment to recognize errant, destructive teachings.

Then Paul imparted a vision for, and a practical understanding of, the functioning gifts and ministries of the Spirit in the local church. The apostle made clear the importance of order in the church, but he also addressed the critical need for a healthy church life—the bonding together of believers in the great calling of being salt and light. All of this combines to make I Corinthians one of the most practical New Testament epistles for establishing a maturing church.

The first problem Paul addressed was the division in the church caused by different factions that followed different spiritual leaders who had visited the church. Some claimed to be followers of Paul, others followed Peter, and still others followed Apollos.

This was not only splitting the Corinthian church apart, but would become a root cause in dividing countless churches throughout this age. Paul's wise counsel on this issue was that these leaders all brought a different aspect of the ministry of God. All of them were needed for the maturing of the church, but we must keep our devotion to the Lord, not to His messengers.

Contrary to what later church leaders would do, Paul's response to the misuse of the gifts of the Spirit was not to have them abandon these gifts, but rather to "earnestly desire" and pursue them. This is noteworthy because throughout church history, the Corinthian church has been known as "the carnal church" and many have blamed their carnal problems on their devotion to the gifts of the Spirit. This is a remarkably contradictory conclusion to the biblical remedy to this problem, which is to desire and pursue the gifts, but to do so decently and with order.

Paul declared in the beginning of the letter (1:6-7) that the testimony of Christ was confirmed in them because they were not lacking in any gift. This linked the functioning of the gifts of the Spirit with the testimony that Christ was among them. The gifts of the Spirit are still Christ doing what He wants to do through His body, the church. To abandon the gifts of the Spirit would be to cease to let Christ do His works through His people.

Much of the teaching in this letter was the result of unique local situations, as was the case with other New Testament epistles. Since most of the shipping between the East and West passed through Corinth, it was one of the most important commercial cities of its day. This was partly due to the fact that Corinth had two seaports—one on the east side on the Aegean Sea and one on the west side facing the Ionian and Adriatic Seas. The city was on a thin strip of land that served as a land bridge. Corinth was a very large, cosmopolitan city for the time with an estimated mixed population of 400,000 people, which were primarily Romans, Greeks, and Jews.

As was the case with many seaports, Corinth was also known for its sensuality and prostitution. The Greek culture was creating unique problems for the church of Corinth, and Paul brought unique counsel to address these problems. One major issue was the impact of the city's chief deity, a Greek goddess named Aphrodite (Venus), the goddess of licentious love. One thousand professional prostitutes served in the temple dedicated to her worship. These prostitutes had their hair shaved to identify them as prostitutes. When some of them were converted to Christ, Paul gave instructions to this church that all women wear head coverings in order to protect these converted prostitutes from discrimination until their hair grew back. This is why the practice of women wearing head coverings was only addressed to the church in Corinth and not to the other New Testament churches. Neither was this a practice found in any other first-century church.

Churches, movements, and even denominations have adopted the requirement of head coverings for women because of Paul's counsel, which was intended only for the Corinthians to address their unique problem. This is an example of how a study of history, culture, and social practices can shed light on some of the texts in Scripture that are not easily understood and prevent the misapplication of them in the formulation of church doctrine.

The spirit of the city influenced the church in other ways as well. Even the power of the Holy Spirit could be seen in a distorted way when viewed through the ideas of paganism that many of these believers formerly held to. Paul brilliantly confronted all of these issues in this letter, alternating rebuke with encouragement and hope. He countered error with sound teaching, elevating truth and wisdom above deception.

Paul also gave the only marriage counseling found in the New Testament. It is noteworthy, because Paul was the one apostle who was not married. This indicates that some problems might be understood better by those who are not so close to them. Paul explained how love is God's counter to perversion and lust. His teaching concluded with possibly the most poetic and insightful exhortation on love ever penned (see Chapter 13).

Paul also opposed the sectarian spirit by teaching on the unity of the church, and how the gifts and ministries function to complement one another, together manifesting the ministry of Christ. He explained that communion is a testimony of this commitment of believers to bond together in unity and how it would counter the food offered to idols. He concluded with a remarkable and comprehensive teaching on the resurrection.

Like the rest of Paul's writings, this letter weaves together a deep understanding of the Old Testament Scriptures with the practical wisdom of the Holy Spirit in addressing unique situations. Therefore, this epistle is one of the most practical for all Christians at any level of maturity. It remains a great aid for individuals and churches in building up a community in unity, love, and dedication to truth in the Spirit of holiness.

NOTES:

PAUL'S FIRST LETTER TO THE
CORINTHIANS
I Corinthians 1

Salutation

1   Paul, called to be an apostle of Jesus Christ by the will of God, and Sosthenes our brother,

2   to the church of God that is at Corinth, to those who are sanctified in Christ Jesus, called to be saints, with all that in every place call upon the name of Jesus Christ our Lord, both theirs and ours.

3   Grace to you, and peace, from God our Father, and from our Lord Jesus Christ.

Our Basic Calling

4   I thank my God always on your behalf, for the grace of God that is given to you by Jesus Christ,

5   so that in every thing you are enriched by Him, in all speech and in all knowledge,

6   even as the testimony of Christ was confirmed in you,

7   so that you are not lacking in any gift, but are waiting for the coming of our Lord Jesus Christ,

8   who will also confirm you until the end, that you may be blameless in the day of our Lord Jesus Christ.

9   God is faithful, by whom you were called into the fellowship of His Son Jesus Christ our Lord.

Call to Unity

10 Now I adjure you, brethren, in the name of our Lord Jesus Christ, that you all agree in what you teach, and that there be no divisions

among you, but that you be perfectly joined together in the same mind and in the same judgment.

11 For it has been declared to me concerning you, my brethren, by those of the house of Chloe, that there are divisions among you.

12 Now all of you say, "I am a follower of Paul;" or "I am a follower of Apollos;" or "I am a follower of Cephas;" or "I am a follower of Christ."

13 Is Christ divided? Was Paul crucified for you? Or were you baptized in the name of Paul?

14 I thank God that I baptized none of you, except for Crispus and Gaius,

15 lest any should say that I had baptized in my name.

16 Now I did also baptize the household of Stephanas, but besides them I do not remember baptizing any other.

17 For Christ did not send me to baptize, but to preach the gospel, not with cleverness of speech, lest the cross of Christ should be made of none effect.

True and False Wisdom

18 For the preaching of the cross is to those who are perishing foolishness, but to those who are saved it is the power of God.

19 For it is written, I will destroy the wisdom of the wise, and will bring to nothing the understanding of the wise and intelligent.

20 Where is the wise man? Where is the scribe? Where is the debater of this age? Has God not made foolish the wisdom of this world?

21 Forsaking the wisdom of God, the world by its wisdom did not come to know God, so it pleased God that by the foolishness of preaching to save those that believe.

The Wisdom of the Call

22 For the Jews require a sign, and the Greeks seek after wisdom,

23 but we preach Christ crucified, which is to the Jews a stumbling block, and to the Greeks foolishness.

24 However, to those who are called, both Jews and Greeks, Christ is the power of God, and the wisdom of God,

25 because the foolishness of God is wiser than men, and the weakness of God is stronger than men.

26 For you see by your calling, brethren, how there are not many wise men after the flesh, not many powerful, not many from the nobility, are called.

27 This is because God has chosen the foolish things of the world to confound the wise, and God has chosen the weak things of the world to confound the things that are mighty,

28 and the base things of the world, and things that are despised, God has chosen. Yes, and things which are not esteemed were chosen to bring to nothing the things that are,

29 so that no flesh could glory in His presence.

30 It is by Him that you are in Christ Jesus, who God made to us wisdom, and righteousness, and sanctification, and redemption.

31 That, just as it is written, **"Let Him that glories, glory in the Lord"** (see Jeremiah 9:24).

Salutation

I Corinthians 1:1-3: Paul's salutations are rich in meaning, encouragement, and purpose. They are examples of how he carefully chose and arranged his words. Because Christ is "The Word," His ministers must be skilled in the use of words and know how to use them and their power.

Our Basic Calling

1:4-9: The gifts of the Spirit are the gifts that Jesus manifested when He walked the earth. Now they are given to His body, the church, as the way that He continues to do His work on earth. The testimony of Christ was confirmed in the church because no gift was lacking, and Jesus could work through them to do anything He did when He walked the earth. Is our

church a testimony that confirms He is still doing His great work on the earth?

Verse 9 states our most basic purpose as Christians—to have fellowship with Jesus. If there is any way to determine true spiritual maturity, it would be by how close we are to the Lord.

Call to Unity

1:10-17: Spiritual maturity is demonstrated by unity. As long as we have divisions in the church, we are still carnal. As stated here, only a devotion to the cross can bring us into unity. If we have built our fellowship on any foundation other than Christ, it will ultimately divide us, not unify us.

True and False Wisdom

1:18-21: To understand the cross is the greatest wisdom. The greatest souls to walk the earth are those who take up their cross daily, living a life of sacrifice for the sake of the gospel. This is true discipleship according to Jesus (see Luke 14:27).

The Wisdom of the Call

1:22-31: Christianity is often accused of being arrogant because it claims to be the only way to God. If Jesus is the Son of God and He came and paid the price for our salvation, then it is supreme arrogance to think we do not need His provision. It is supreme arrogance to think we can make it through life on our own. For this reason, to believe the gospel is true, yet allow for other ways to God, is the greatest affront to God and the cross. The supreme arrogance of man is to believe that we do not need God. For anyone to think that Christ would have suffered what He did if there was another way, is an ultimate affront to the very intelligence of God. In truth, those who reject Christ and His atonement are guilty of the ultimate arrogance, not to mention a basic heresy.

NOTES:

Paul's First Letter To The
CORINTHIANS
I Corinthians 2

The Power of the Gospel

1 When I came to you, brethren, I did not come with an excellence of speech, or of wisdom, declaring to you the testimony of God.

2 I determined to know nothing among you except Jesus Christ, and Him crucified.

3 I was with you in weakness, and in fear, and in much trembling,

4 and my speech and my preaching was not with enticing words of man's wisdom, but in demonstration of the Spirit, and power,

5 so that your faith would not be based on the wisdom of men, but on the power of God.

Wisdom for the Mature

6 Even so, we speak wisdom among those who are mature. Yet it is not the wisdom of this world, nor of the rulers of this world, but the wisdom of the age to come.

7 We speak the wisdom of God in a mystery, even the hidden wisdom that God ordained before the world to our glory.

8 None of the rulers of this world knew this wisdom, because if they had known it they would not have crucified the Lord of glory.

9 But as it is written, **"Eye has not seen, nor ear heard, neither has it entered into the heart of man, the things which God has prepared for those who love him" (see Isaiah 64:4, 65:17).**

Spiritual Language

10 God has revealed them to us by His Spirit, because the Spirit searches all things, even the deep things of God.

11 For what man knows the things that are truly in a man, except the spirit of man that is in him? Even so, the things of God no man knows except for the Spirit of God.

12 Now we have not received the spirit of the world, but the Spirit that is from God, so that we might know the things that are freely given to us by God.

13 These things we also speak, not in the words taught by man's wisdom, but as the Holy Spirit teaches, comparing spiritual things with spiritual words.

14 The natural man does not receive the things of the Spirit of God because they are foolishness to him. Neither can he understand them because they are spiritually discerned.

15 He that is spiritual can understand all things, yet he cannot be understood by any man.

16 For who has known the mind of the Lord, that he may instruct Him? Even so, we have the mind of Christ.

The Power of the Gospel

I Corinthians 2:1-5: Much effort is put into intellectually persuading people so they will come to Christ. To debate the crucial issues of life is not wrong, but before anyone can be converted, the Holy Spirit must convict them of sin and their desperate need for the atoning work of the cross as the only remedy for their guilt. "The cross is the power of God." It is the cross that we must preach, and it is the cross that we must demonstrate by living our lives for Him and not just ourselves.

Wisdom for the Mature

2:6-9: The wisdom of God is as far above human reasoning as the rest of the universe is to the earth. Even so, God came to earth to impart to man the knowledge of His ways so that we might walk with Him. Therefore, pursuing His ways and His wisdom is the greatest devotion of man. As we mature in Christ, we begin to perceive the unfathomable wisdom of

His ways. This is a basis for the highest fellowship among the mature in Christ.

Spiritual Language

2:10-16: The reason the Holy Spirit is given is to lead us into all truth and to lead us to Jesus, who is the Truth. Our goal should be to see the world and every situation through His eyes and to act towards them the way that He would.

In verse 16, Paul said "we" have the mind of Christ, not "I." We each "see in part and know in part," so as we come together in unity, we have His mind. This too is the wisdom of God—a wisdom that keeps those who receive it humble before Him and one another. He has composed His body so that we need one another and must, therefore, love one another.

NOTES:

PAUL'S FIRST LETTER TO THE
CORINTHIANS
I Corinthians 3

The Evidence of Immaturity

1   I, brethren, could not speak to you as to those who are spiritual, but I had to speak as to those yet carnal, even as to babes in Christ.

2   I have fed you with milk, and not with meat, because until now you were not able to bear it, neither are you able to now.

3   For you are still carnal, which is proven by the envy, strife, and divisions among you. In this way you are still carnal, and still walk as mere men.

4   For while one says, "I am of Paul"; and another, "I am of Apollos," are you not still carnal?

5   Who then is Paul, and who is Apollos, but ministers through whom you believed, even as the Lord gave the ability to every man?

6   I have planted, Apollos watered, but God gave the increase.

7   So then neither is he that plants significant, neither is he that waters, but it is God who gives the increase.

8   Now he that plants and he that waters are in unity, and every man will receive his own reward according to his own labor.

9   For we are laborers together with God, and you are God's field, God's building.

The Right Foundation

10   According to the grace of God that has been given to me, as a wise master builder I have laid the foundation, and another has built upon it. Let every man take heed how he builds on it.

11   For no other foundation can be laid than that which is laid, which is Jesus Christ.

12 Now if any man builds upon this foundation with gold, silver, precious stones, or wood, hay, and stubble,

13 every man's work will be made manifest for what it is. The day is coming that will reveal it, because it will be revealed by fire. The fire will test every man's work to determine its quality.

14 If any man's work remains after the test, he will receive a reward.

15 If any man's work is burned up, he will suffer loss, but he himself will be saved, even though it will be through the fire.

His Temple

16 Do you not know that you are the temple of God, and that the Spirit of God dwells in you?

17 If any man defiles the temple of God, he will be destroyed by God, because the temple of God is holy, and you are the temple.

18 Let no man deceive himself. If any man among you presumes to be wise in this world, let him consider himself to be a fool, and then he will have an opportunity to become wise.

19 For the wisdom of this world is foolishness with God. For it is written, **"He takes the wise in their own craftiness" (see Job 5:13).**

20 And again, **"The Lord knows the thoughts of the wise, that they are vain" (see Psalm 94:11).**

21 Therefore let no man glory in men. For all things are yours.

22 Whether Paul, or Apollos, or Cephas, or the world, or life, or death, or things present, or things to come, they are yours,

23 and you are Christ's; and Christ is God's.

The Evidence of Immaturity

I Corinthians 3:1-9: The most basic evidence of spiritual immaturity is division with other members of the body of Christ. In His last night on earth as a man, one of the primary things Jesus prayed for was unity among His people (see John 17). This is one of the greatest desires of the Son of God. Therefore, how could we fail to make it one of ours? Having

divisions, which is merely the result of running from the process of working differences out with other believers, is evidence of spiritual immaturity and carnality. The process of working out our differences so that they do not turn into offenses and bitterness that defile many is required for maturity in Christ.

As we see in this text, the primary source of division in the Corinthian church was the tendency to follow individual men of God, rather than understanding that just as we see in part and know in part, each of these leaders has a part, yet the whole is Christ Himself. When we begin to see Christ, it is not possible to be overly restricted by only following one person or part of the body. We must give proper honor to all.

In verse 9, Paul uses two different metaphors for what we are—God's field and His building. We are also referred to in Scripture as God's temple, His body, His bride, His army, His holy nation, His priests, light, salt, and His sons and daughters. As individuals, we are also many things, just like I am a husband, father, pastor, writer, conference speaker, pilot, and so on. Therefore, it is important that we know what we are to do at any given time. So it is with the church. What is God emphasizing and building in us right now?

The Right Foundation

3:10-15: The Lord sends fire to test every work, so we should never think it is a strange thing when the trials come. Rather, we are to embrace them as being necessary to challenge the quality of what is being built. That which is truly precious will only be purified by the trials, and that which is not will be consumed, which is what we all should want.

His Temple

3:16-23: This is one of the most remarkable of all revelations in the New Testament—that we have actually been chosen to be God's dwelling place, His temple. If we were told that the President was going to visit us and stay for a week in our house, wouldn't we clean our houses like never before? Some people would paint, others might buy new furniture, and some would probably even buy a new house just for such a visit. Yet someone greater than the President has come to live in us. How much more should we be devoted to cleaning and preparing a place for Him in our hearts? How different would we be if we spent as much time cleaning and grooming our inner man as we do the outer man? What would we be like if we spent as much time getting our inner man in shape as we do the outer man?

NOTES:

PAUL'S FIRST LETTER TO THE
CORINTHIANS
I Corinthians 4

Unrighteous Judgment

1 So let a man acknowledge us as the ministers of Christ, and stewards of the mysteries of God.

2 Moreover it is required of stewards that they are trustworthy.

3 However, with me it is a very small thing that I should be judged by you, or by any human court. In fact, I do not even judge myself.

4 For I know of nothing against myself, yet I am not by this acquitted, but He that judges me is the Lord.

5 Therefore judge nothing before the time, but wait until the Lord comes who will both bring to light the things hidden in darkness, and will make manifest the counsels of every heart. Then every man will have the praise that is due him from God.

6 My brethren, I have attributed these things to myself and to Apollos for your sakes, so that you might learn through us not to think of men more than that which is written, so that no one of you is exalted in your own eyes above one another.

7 For who makes you to differ from another? What do you have that you did not receive? Now if you received it, why do you boast in yourself as if you had not received it?

8 Now you are full, now you are rich. You have reigned as kings without us! I would to God that you did reign so that we also might reign with you.

Apostolic Humility

9 I think that God has set forth us, the apostles, as last of all, as those appointed to death. We have been made a spectacle to the world, to angels, and to men.

10 We are fools for Christ's sake, but you are wise in Christ. We are weak, but you are strong. You are honorable, but we are despised.

11 Even to this present time we are hungry, thirsty, naked, are buffeted, and have no certain dwelling place.

12 We labor, working with our own hands. Even though we are reviled, we bless. We are persecuted, and we suffer patiently.

13 When we are defamed, we are conciliatory. We are made as the filth of the world, and are considered the lowest of all things to this day.

A Father's Appeal

14 I do not write these things to shame you, but as my beloved sons I warn you.

15 For though you have innumerable teachers in Christ, you do not have many fathers. In Christ Jesus I am the one who has begotten you through the gospel.

16 Therefore, I beseech you, to be an imitator of me.

17 For this cause I have sent to you Timothy, who is my beloved son, and is faithful in the Lord. He will bring to your remembrance my ways that are in Christ, as I teach everywhere in every church.

18 Now some have become arrogant, thinking that I would not come to you.

19 However, I will come to you shortly, if the Lord wills, and will expose not just the speech of those who are arrogant, but their power.

20 For the kingdom of God does not consist of words, but power.

21 What would you choose? Shall I come to you with a rod, or in love, and in the spirit of meekness?

Unrighteous Judgment

I Corinthians 4:1-8: A basic requirement for leadership in the church is being trustworthy, which means to be worthy of trust. Trust is something that must be earned and can never be assumed. Do we have a track record that is worthy of trust?

There is a way to judge by the Holy Spirit, even when we lack awareness. He is the Spirit of Truth and will lead us into all truth, if we follow Him. Paul sought to have the Spirit examine him rather than try to judge himself because he knew how easily deceived we can be in regard to ourselves.

Apostolic Humility

4:9-13: New Testament apostles were universally assailed, ridiculed, demeaned, and slandered. So are true apostles today. To lead on such a level, all hell knows you and is intent on stopping you any way it can. The Lord uses persecution to purify His people, especially His leaders. The more humble they remain, the more grace and authority they can receive.

A Father's Appeal

4:14-21: It is still true today that we have many teachers, but not many fathers. We often think of spiritual fathers as being older, more experienced men of God. However, just as in the natural, most men become fathers when they are young—it is the same in the Spirit. Being a spiritual father has less to do with age and life experience than with the ability to reproduce. How many ministries are reproducing their ministry in others? How many Christians are making disciples and not just converts?

The power that God demonstrates through His people is power over all the works of the devil, including disease. His power includes miracles as a demonstration of the authority of the kingdom of God over any condition on the earth. The ultimate power of the kingdom of God is the power of life, reproduction, and fruit that multiplies, not just the power of persuasive words.

NOTES:

Paul's First Letter To The
CORINTHIANS
I Corinthians 5

Confronting Immorality

1 It is commonly reported that there is immorality among you, and such as does not even exist among the Gentiles, that one would have his father's wife.

2 You are arrogant about this, and have not even mourned so that he who has done this deed might be put out from among you.

3 For I, though absent in body, but present in spirit, have judged the one who has done this deed as though I were present.

4 In the name of our Lord Jesus Christ, when you are gathered together, and my spirit with you, in the power of our Lord Jesus Christ,

5 deliver such a one over to Satan for the destruction of his flesh, so that his spirit may be saved in the day of the Lord Jesus.

6 Your glorying is not good. Do you not know that a little leaven leavens the whole lump?

Unleavened Bread

7 Therefore purge out the old leaven that you may be a new lump of dough, because you are to be unleavened. For Christ, our Passover, has been sacrificed for us.

8 Therefore let us keep the feast, not with old leaven, neither with the leaven of malice and wickedness, but with the unleavened bread of sincerity and truth.

9 I wrote to you in a letter not to keep company with the immoral.

10 Yet this does not mean with the immoral of this world, or with the covetous, or extortionist, or with idolaters, for then you would have to go out of the world.

11 I have written to you not to keep company with any man that is called a brother who is immoral, or covetous, or an idolater, or a fault-finder, or a drunkard, or an extortionist. With such a one do not even eat.

12 For what have I to do with judging those who are outside of the church? Do you not judge those that are within?

13 Those who are without God judges. Therefore put out the wicked person from among yourselves.

Confronting Immorality

I Corinthians 5:1-6: Immorality is a devastating sin that can spread and infect others, destroying the core unit of society, the family, and all other relationships. Therefore, this basic enemy of humanity cannot be tolerated in the body of Christ. This does not mean that when one stumbles they must be cut off, but if they do not repent, then it is a danger to the whole body. When someone begins to boast about their sin, they are close to developing a hardened heart from which few recover. The radical action of turning this sinner over to Satan for the destruction of his flesh was done in order to save his soul. This action brought repentance in the church at Corinth and a healthy fear of God and of sin, as we will read in Paul's next letter to the Corinthians.

Unleavened Bread

5:7-13: In Scripture, leaven is used as a metaphor for both sin and wickedness, which is lawlessness and legalism (Jesus called the teachings of the Pharisees "leaven"). These are the two ditches that are on either side of the path of life. The Feast of Unleavened Bread is still celebrated by Jews as part of the Passover Feast to remember that Israel left Egypt in such haste that their bread did not have time to leaven. This speaks of how we keep our bread, or life, free from what leaven represents—we keep moving and growing in Christ with such energy and speed that neither sin, nor wickedness, nor legalism have time to take hold in our lives. Those who stop growing in Christ, those who depart from the ever flowing River of Life, will inevitably drift into either lawlessness or legalism.

Many people have wrongly interpreted Jesus' statement "do not judge lest you be judged" (see Matthew 7:1-5) as an absolute that we should never judge anyone for anything. First, to take what Jesus said out of context like this is to change the meaning of what He said. He did not say that we should not judge, but that we should first remove the log in our own eye before we try to remove the speck from someone else's. There are exhortations in Scripture, like this one, that make the failure to use righteous judgment a basic failure of our responsibility. Unrighteous judgment is evil and will lead to evil, but unrighteous judgment is what fills the vacuum created by a lack of righteous judgment. Righteous judgment must be firm and uncompromising of biblical standards of righteousness, but they must also have the redemptive purpose of saving souls, not condemning them.

NOTES:

PAUL'S FIRST LETTER TO THE
CORINTHIANS

I Corinthians 6

The Call for Judges

1   Do any of you who have a dispute against another dare to go to court before the heathen and not before the saints?

2   Do you not know that the saints will judge the world? If the world will be judged by you, are you not worthy to judge these small matters?

3   Do you not know that you will judge angels? How much more the things pertaining to this life?

4   If then you have need of a judgment for things pertaining to this life, do you make them judges who are the least esteemed in the church?

5   I say this to your shame! Is it so that there is not one wise man among you? Is there not one that will be able to judge disputes between his brethren?

6   But when brother goes to court against a brother, and that before the unbelievers, it is already a defeat for you, because you go to court with one another.

7   It would be better to just accept the wrong. Why do you not rather suffer yourselves to be defrauded than to make this even worse mistake?

8   Instead you do wrong, and defraud, your brethren.

Call to Sanctification

9   Do you not know that the unrighteous will not inherit the kingdom of God? Do not be deceived, neither will fornicators, idolaters, adulterers, effeminate, homosexuals,

10 thieves, covetous, drunkards, revilers, extortionists, inherit the kingdom of God.

11 Such were some of you, but you have been cleansed, you are sanctified, you are justified in the name of the Lord Jesus by the Spirit of our God.

12 All things may be lawful to me, but that does not make them expedient. All things may be lawful for me, but I will not be brought under the power of any.

13 Food is for the belly, and the belly for food, but God will destroy both it and them. Now the body is not for fornication, but for the Lord, and the Lord for the body.

14 God has both raised up the Lord, and will also raise us up by His own power.

A Holy Temple

15 Do you not know that your bodies are the members of Christ? Will I then take the members of Christ and make them the members of a harlot? God forbid!

16 What? Do you not know that he who is joined to a harlot becomes one with her? For He said that the two will become one flesh.

17 Likewise, he that is joined to the Lord is one spirit with Him.

18 Flee fornication! Every sin that a man does is outside of the body, except he that commits fornication, sins against his own body.

19 Do you not know that your body is the temple of the Holy Spirit which is in you, which you have from God, and you are not your own?

20 For you have been bought with a price. Therefore glorify God in your body, and in your spirit, which are God's.

The Call for Judges

I Corinthians 6:1-8: New Testament church government was modeled after the Old Testament government of Israel. In Israel, elders were primarily judges, which was also a basic duty of New Testament church elders. As Paul writes here, "I

say this to your shame." The failure of church elders to be the judges they are called to be is a primary reason why there is so much shame in the body of Christ. If we do not have righteous judges and righteous judgment, we will have unrighteous judges and unrighteous judgment to fill the void.

Call to Sanctification

6:9-14: The Word of God is clear that if we continue in the corruption of sin, we will not inherit the kingdom of God. Those who try to rationalize or explain away such clear teachings in Scripture are obviously steeped in deception and risk ultimate jeopardy. Love would never compromise these teachings because such compromise could put those in eternal jeopardy who rationalize away what God has called sin and continue in it.

A Holy Temple

6:15-20: Every other sin we are exhorted to resist, except for sexual immorality, which we are told to flee from. This is what Joseph did (see Genesis 39). Though for a time it looked as if he had made a great mistake because it landed him in prison, Joseph's unyielding righteousness was the pathway to his high calling. So it is with us.

NOTES:

PAUL'S FIRST LETTER TO THE
CORINTHIANS
I Corinthians 7

Responsibilities in Marriage

1   Now concerning the things about which you wrote to me, it is good when a man can go without touching a woman.

2   Nevertheless, to avoid immorality let every man have his own wife, and let every woman have her own husband.

3   Let the husband render to his wife the benevolence that she is due, and likewise also the wife to the husband.

4   The wife does not have authority over her own body, but the husband does. Likewise the husband does not have authority over his own body, but the wife does.

5   Do not defraud one another in your relationship, except for times when you both consent so that you may give yourselves to fasting and prayer. Then come together again so that Satan is not able to tempt you because of your negligence.

6   I speak this as a concession, and not as a commandment.

7   I would rather that all men were even as I am, but every man has his gift from God, and each one is different.

8   I therefore recommend to the unmarried and widows that it is good for them if they abide *alone* even as I do.

9   However, if they are without self-control let them marry. It is better to marry than to burn *with lust.*

10 To the married we have a command that is not just from me, but from the Lord, "Let the wife not depart from her husband.

11 "But if she does depart, let her remain unmarried, or be reconciled to her husband. Let not the husband put away his wife."

An Unbelieving Spouse

12 To the rest I give my own counsel, not a commandment from the Lord. If any brother has a wife that is not a believer, and she is content to dwell with him, let him not put her away.

13 If a woman has a husband that is not a believer, and if he is content to dwell with her, let her not leave him.

14 For the unbelieving husband is sanctified by the wife. The unbelieving wife is sanctified by the husband, otherwise your children would be unclean, but now they are holy.

15 If the unbelieving *spouse* departs, let them depart. A brother or a sister is not under bondage in such cases.

16 God has called us to peace, so what do you know, O wife, whether you will save your husband? Or what do you know, O man, whether you will save your wife?

Contentment

17 As God has distributed gifts to every man, and as the Lord has called every one, so let him walk. This is what I have commanded in all the churches.

18 Is any man called while circumcised? Let him not become uncircumcised. Is any called in un-circumcision? Let him not be circumcised.

19 Circumcision is nothing, and un-circumcision is nothing, but obeying the precepts of God is what matters.

20 Let every man abide in the same calling in which he was called.

21 Were you called while being a servant? Do not be concerned about it, but if you can become free, do so.

22 For he that is called in the Lord, and is a servant, is the Lord's freeman. Likewise, he that is called when free is Christ's servant.

23 You were bought with a price, so do not become the servants of men if you are free.

24 Brethren, let every man abide with God in the condition in which he is called.

25 Now concerning virgins, I have no commandment from the Lord. This I give as my judgment, as one that has obtained mercy from the Lord to be faithful.

26 I think that it is good because of the present distress for a man to remain as he is.

27 Are you bound to a wife? Do not seek to be loosed. Are you without a wife? Do not seek a wife.

28 If you marry you have not sinned. If a virgin marries, she has not sinned. Nevertheless, such will have trouble in the flesh that I would spare you.

29 This I say, brethren, the time is short. It will be that both they that have wives will be as though they had none,

30 and they that weep, as though they did not weep, and those who rejoice, as though they did not rejoice, and they that purchase goods as though they possessed nothing.

31 Those who make full use of this world will not be able to continue to do so as the ways of this world will pass away.

32 I would have you to be without such concerns. He that is not married cares for the things that belong to the Lord, how he may please the Lord.

33 He that is married cares for the things that are of the world, how he may please his wife.

34 There is a difference also between a wife and a virgin. The unmarried woman cares for the things of the Lord, how she may be holy both in body and in spirit. She that is married cares for the things of the world, how she may please her husband.

Freedom to Choose

35 This I speak for your own profit, not that I may cast a restraint upon you, but so that you may devote yourself to that which is honorable, and that you may attend to the Lord without distraction.

36 If any man thinks that he is not doing right toward his virgin daughter, if she passes the age of youth, he should do what the needs require. Let him do what he will, he does not sin: let her marry.

37 Nevertheless he that stands steadfast in his heart, and is not compelled by circumstances, but has power over his own will, and has so decreed in his heart that he will keep his daughter a virgin, does well.

38 So then he that gives her in marriage does well, but he that does not give her in marriage does better.

39 The wife is bound by the law as long as her husband lives, but if her husband dies, she is at liberty to be married to whom she will, but only in the Lord.

40 However, in my judgment, she will be happier if she abides alone, and I think that I have the Spirit of God in this matter.

Responsibilities in Marriage

I Corinthians 7:1-11: It is interesting that the only marriage counselor in The Bible is Paul, who was not married. Sometimes one who is not in a situation may be able to see into it more clearly than those who are. Nevertheless, Paul's counsel is canon Scripture, and it is sound, practical wisdom.

An Unbelieving Spouse

7:12-16: Some of the most perpetually trying circumstances that believers can encounter are the result of having an un-believing spouse. However, great good can come from this situation when one endures and sees it as an opportunity to win the unbeliever to the Lord. Also, embracing trials opens up great opportunity to be conformed to the image of Christ. Finally, consider what His bride, the church, has been like for Him to endure.

In verse 15, the apostle writes that if an unbelieving spouse leaves a believer, then, in such cases, the believer is "not in bondage." This is almost universally interpreted that, in such cases, the believer is free to remarry, because the only bond-age that applies here is to the spouse. Therefore, if a spouse is free from the marriage because the other has left them, they are free to remarry.

Contentment

7:17-34: The apostle makes it clear that he counsels Christians not to get married. This may have been 1) because of the present distress and 2) to secure undistracted devotion to the Lord. There have been long periods of relative peace for Christians in certain places and times that could seem to eliminate Paul's reason #1. However, reason #2 is always valid. Even so, taking his whole counsel, even in difficult times it is much better for one to marry if they do not have self-control. There is another valid reason that Paul does not address here. God created man and woman with an attraction for each other. Romance is a special gift that enables us to grasp His love for His bride, the church. This is a gift to be appreciated and honored. There is no Cupid, but God Himself seems to enjoy creating romance between couples, and when this happens, marriage is the right course.

Freedom to Choose

7:35-40: Again, there are principles, and there are laws. There are exceptions to principles but not to laws. In his counsel about marriage, Paul shares basic principles that are generally true, but with great wisdom, he promotes freedom with his counsel. This is the Spirit of the New Covenant. There are commandments in the New Covenant we must obey, but with much of the teaching, there is a freedom that compels us to search our hearts and seek the heart of the Lord, which is one of the great methods of drawing us closer to God.

NOTES:

Paul's First Letter To The
CORINTHIANS
I Corinthians 8

Things Sacrificed to Idols

1 Now about things offered to idols, we all have knowledge. Knowledge makes arrogant, but love edifies.

2 If any man thinks that he knows anything entirely, he does not yet know what he should know.

3 If any man loves God, the same is known by Him.

4 Concerning the eating of those things that are offered as a sacrifice to idols, we know that an idol is nothing in the world, and that there is no other god but one.

5 For though there are many so-called gods, whether in heaven or in earth (as there are many gods, and many lords),

6 but to us there is but one God, who is the Father *of all*, from whom are all things *originated*, and we are in Him. There is also one Lord, Jesus Christ, by whom came all things, and we are from Him.

Protecting the Weak

7 However, not every man has this knowledge, because some who have a conscience about the idol eat it as a thing offered to an idol, and their conscience being weak, is defiled.

8 Food does not commend us to God. If we eat, we are not better, and if we do not eat, we are not worse.

9 Be careful unless by any means this liberty of yours becomes a stumbling block to those who are weak.

10 If a man sees you which have this knowledge sit for a meal in the idol's temple, will not the conscience of him who is weak be emboldened to eat those things that are offered to idols?

11 Should it be that through your knowledge the weak brother perishes, one for whom Christ died?

12 When you so sin against the brethren, and wound their weak conscience, you sin against Christ.

13 Therefore, if eating meat offends my brother, I will not eat it while the present age lasts, in order not to offend my brother.

Things Sacrificed to Idols

I Corinthians 8:1-6: Idols in biblical times were often images that people worshiped. However, today an idol is anything we give devotion to or trust in more than God. Idols can be money, our profession, associations, other people, or even the church. Not that these things are evil, yet they become an evil devotion when our allegiance to them eclipses our allegiance to God.

Protecting the Weak

8:7-13: This text speaks to specific situations that existed at the time the epistle was written, but the principle still applies to us today. Since we have liberty to do things that are not specifically forbidden, we need to be careful not to use this liberty in a way that could cause those who are immature, or not strong enough to handle this liberty, to stumble. Love and concern for the weak should always trump liberty when we have to choose between the two.

NOTES:

PAUL'S FIRST LETTER TO THE
CORINTHIANS
I Corinthians 9

Paul Defends His Apostleship

1   Am I not an apostle? Am I not free? Have I not seen Jesus Christ our Lord? Are you not my work in the Lord?

2   If I am not an apostle to others, certainly I am to you, for you are the seal of my apostleship in the Lord.

3   My answer to those who examine me is this,

4   do we not have the authority to eat and to drink?

5   Do we not have the authority to take a *Christian* sister as a wife, just as the other apostles, the brethren of the Lord, and Cephas?

6   Or do only Barnabas and I not have the right not to work to support ourselves?

Provision for Workers

7 Who goes to war at his own expense? Who plants a vineyard, but does not eat the fruit of it? Or who feeds a flock, and does not partake of the milk of the flock?

8 Do I say these things as a man? Does not the law also say the same?

9 For it is written in the law of Moses, **"You shall not muzzle the mouth of the ox that treads out the corn" (see Deuteronomy 25:4).** Does God take this care just for oxen?

10 Does He say this for our sakes? It is for our sakes. No doubt it is also for us that this is also written that he who plows should plow in hope of partaking of the crop, and he that threshes should also be a partaker of the harvest.

11 If we have sown in you spiritual things, is it too much to expect that we will reap natural things?

12 If others are partakers of this right with you, should we not be also? Nevertheless we have not used this right, but suffer all things that we do so that we will not hinder the gospel of Christ.

13 Do you not know that those who minister in the holy things live off of those things in the temple? Those who serve at the altar are partakers with the altar.

14 Even so, the Lord has ordained that those who preach the gospel should make their living from the gospel.

15 I have not used these things, and neither have I written these things because I intend to do so, for I would rather die than have any man make my boasting invalid.

Responsibility of the Call

16 For though I preach the gospel, I have nothing to glory in, for I am compelled to do so. Yes, it would be woe to me if I did not preach the gospel!

17 For if I do this thing willingly, I have a reward, but if against my will, and a dispensation of the gospel is committed to me,

18 what is my reward then? It is my devotion that when I preach I may present the gospel of Christ without charge so that I do not abuse my right in the gospel.

19 For though I am free from all men, yet have I made myself a servant to all so that I might win more.

Winning Other Cultures

20 It is for this reason that to the Jews I became as a Jew, that I might win the Jews. To those who are under the Law, I became as one under the Law, so that I might gain those who are under the Law.

21 To those who are without law, I became as one without law, (not being without the law of God, but under the law to Christ,) that I might gain those who are without law.

22 To the weak I became as weak, that I might gain the weak. I became as all things to all men, that I might by all means save some.

23 This I do for the gospel's sake, that I might be partaker of this harvest with you.

Running the Race

24 Do you not know that those who run in a race, all run, but only one receives the prize? So run in a way that you may obtain *the* prize.

25 Every man that strives for mastery in a sport is temperate in all things. Now they do it to obtain a corruptible crown, but we an incorruptible one.

26 I therefore run to win, not as one who has an uncertain goal. When I fight I do not do it to beat the air.

27 For this reason I keep my body under control, and bring it into subjection, lest by any means, even though I have preached to others, I myself should be disqualified.

Paul Defends His Apostleship

I Corinthians 9:1-6: Paul made a brief but remarkable defense of his apostleship, which also defines the nature of an authentic apostle. The first requirement is that they must have seen the Lord. Does this mean that the Lord still appears to men? Yes, He is the same today as He was then, and He relates to His church in the same way. Because of the nature and authority of the apostolic ministry, apostles are commissioned directly by the Lord just as we see in the New Testament.

Next, we see that the fruit of Paul's apostleship was actually the very people who were challenging his authority as an apostle. Paul bore fruit that proved who he was, and the fruit was challenging him! This is not uncommon, as those who are closest to their leaders can become so familiar with them that they lose perspective and respect for them. True apostolic ministry, and indeed all ministries, can be the most thankless of jobs, particularly if we are seeking the approval of men. For this reason, ministry must be done for the sake of the Lord, not for acknowledgement by men.

Paul acknowledged here that he was not an apostle to everyone, which gives us an important insight into the range of apostolic authority. All ministry has spheres of authority. Paul had been called specifically to the Gentiles, just as Peter was called to the Jews. Even the great Apostle Paul would not presume to have authority over the work of another, but he would come to them in the capacity they determined, not his own.

Even though there is an obvious limit to apostolic ministry, the authority of Paul's letters would and should be accepted throughout the body of Christ as canon Scripture. This is because he wrote universal truth and universal wisdom that applies to all.

Provision for Workers

9:7-15: Support of those who serve in the ministry of the church seems to have been a challenge throughout the church age. Some people believe in keeping those who serve in ministry in virtual poverty, while others have gone to the other extreme and made the ministry a source for becoming wealthy. Both of these extremes can be an affront to the work of the gospel. The wisdom of God is stated as, "let your moderation be known unto all men" (see Philippians 4:5 KJV).

Responsibility of the Call

9:16-19: There is a paradox to the call—we are slaves, and yet we are kings. We are compelled to preach because of responsibility, yet we cannot help but preach out of love for the people and the truth we have been entrusted with, as well as love for the One who entrusted this ministry to us.

Winning Other Cultures

9:20-23: Paul did not become all things to all men out of the fear of man, but out of love for them. This difference can keep us from compromising the truth and yet not be a stumbling block to those who might receive it.

Running the Race

9:24-27: To hear the words "Well done, good and faithful servant" (see Matthew 25:23) on that great judgment day will be a greater reward than any human accolade could ever be. The championships we earn in this life can gain us fame for a lifetime, but what we do for the Lord will last for eternity.

NOTES:

Paul's First Letter To The
CORINTHIANS
I Corinthians 10

Israel's Journey is Our Map

1   My brethren, I do not want you to be ignorant of how our fathers were under the cloud, and all passed through the sea,

2   and were all baptized into Moses in the cloud and in the sea.

3   They all ate the same spiritual food,

4   and drank the same spiritual drink, because they drank from the spiritual Rock that followed them, and that Rock was Christ.

5   However, with many of them God was not pleased, so they perished in the wilderness.

6   Now these things are written as examples for us so that we would not lust after evil things like they did.

7   And so that we would not be idolaters, as some of them were. As it is written, **"The people sat down to eat and drink, and rose up to play" (see Exodus 32:4,6).**

8   Neither let us commit fornication, as some of them did, and in one day twenty-three thousand fell.

9   Neither let us tempt Christ, as some of them did, and were destroyed by serpents.

10   Do not complain, as some of them did, and were destroyed of the destroyer.

11   Now all these things happened to them as a type, and they were written for our instruction upon whom the end of the age has come.

Temptations

12 Therefore let him that thinks that he stands take heed lest he fall.

13 No temptation has come upon you but such as is common to man, and God is faithful not to allow you to be tempted above that you are able to endure. Along with the temptation He will also provide a way to escape, that you may be able to bear it.

14 Therefore, my dearly beloved, flee from idolatry.

15 I speak as to wise men; you judge what I say.

Communion

16 The cup of blessing that we bless, is it not the communion we have in the blood of Christ? The bread that we break, is it not the communion we have in the body of Christ?

17 For we, though we are many, are one bread and one body, because we are all partakers of the one bread.

18 Consider Israel after the flesh: are not they that eat of the sacrifices partakers of the altar?

19 What do I say then? That the idol is anything, or that which is offered in sacrifice to idols is anything?

20 But I say, that the things the Gentiles sacrifice, they sacrifice to devils, and not to God, and I do not want you to have fellowship with devils.

21 You cannot drink the cup of the Lord, and the cup of devils. You cannot be partakers of the Lord's table, and of the table of devils.

22 Can we provoke the Lord to jealousy? Are we stronger than He is?

23 All things are lawful for me, but all things are not expedient. All things are lawful for me, but not all things edify.

24 Let no man seek his own, but let every man seek the welfare of others.

Meat Sacrificed to Idols

25 Whatever is sold in the meat market eat, asking no question for conscience sake.

26 **"For the earth is the Lord's, and the fullness thereof"** (see Psalm 24:1, 50:12).

27 If unbelievers ask you to a feast, and you are willing to go, eat whatever is set before you, asking no questions for conscience sake.

28 However, if anyone says to you, "This is offered in sacrifice to idols," do not eat it for his sake, and for conscience sake.

29 Their conscience, I say, not your own. So why is my liberty judged by another man's conscience?

30 For if I by grace am a partaker, why am I reviled for that for which I have given thanks for?

31 Therefore, whether you eat, or drink, or whatever you do, do it for the glory of God.

32 Give no one a chance to be offended, neither the Jews, nor the Gentiles, nor the church of God.

33 Do as I do seeking to please all men in all things. I do not do this to seek my own profit, but the profit of the many, that they may be saved.

Israel's Journey is Our Map

I Corinthians 10:1-11: This text explains how the journey of Israel through the wilderness is a prophecy for the church at the end of the age. Church history parallels Israel's in many ways. The history of Israel provides a remarkable and accurate map for New Covenant sojourners. Like the Israelites, before we can attain the promises we have received from God, we must go through a wilderness that is usually the opposite of what we have been promised. This wilderness is intended to prepare us to rule well over our promised land when we do possess it.

The first generation of Israel to leave Egypt stumbled over the lessons that Paul highlights here, causing them not to inherit their promises. With such a clear warning as this, we must be far more dull spiritually and hard of heart than they were if we stumble over the same things.

Temptations

10:12-15: Temptations are not created by God, but they are allowed by Him to test us to see if we will walk in His ways, just as the wilderness tested Israel. The Lord also promises that we will never be tempted beyond what we can endure. Therefore, when we feel we are getting close to where we cannot endure any longer, we know that we are near the end of the trial. Don't give up!

Communion

10:16-24: We are told that the ritual of communion is our common-union in the blood and body of Christ. We are members of one another. Therefore, what we eat, drink, and do should be weighed in consideration of whether it will cause other weaker members in the body to stumble. Love should dictate our actions more than desire.

Meat Sacrificed to Idols

10-25-33: Love would never esteem liberty over helping others not to stumble.

NOTES:

PAUL'S FIRST LETTER TO THE
CORINTHIANS

I Corinthians 11

Headship

1 Follow me as I follow Christ.

2 Now I commend you, my brethren, that you remember me in all things, and keep the ordinances just as I delivered them to you.

3 I would have you know that the head of every man is Christ, and the head of the woman is the man, and the head of Christ is God.

4 Every man praying or prophesying, having his head covered, dishonors his head.

5 Every woman that prays, or prophesies, with her head uncovered dishonors her head as if her head were shaven.

6 For if the woman is not covered let her also be shorn. If it is a shame for a woman to be shorn or shaven, let her be covered.

7 A man should not cover his head because he is the image and glory of God, but the woman is the glory of the man.

8 For the man did not come from the woman, but the woman came from the man.

9 Neither was the man created for the woman, but the woman for the man.

10 For this cause the woman should have authority over her head because of the angels.

11 However, no man can come into being without the woman, neither the woman without the man, as the Lord has established.

12 For as the woman is from the man, even so is the man also from the woman, but all things are from God.

13 Judge for yourselves; is it right that a woman pray to God uncovered?

14 Does not even nature itself teach you that, if a man h·
is a shame to him?

15 If a woman has long hair, it is a glory to her, bec·
given to her for a covering.

16 If any man is to be contentious over this matter, we have no such
custom, neither the churches of God.

A Second Call to Unity

17 Now this I declare, that I do not commend you because you do not
come together for the better, but for the worse.

18 First of all, when you come together in the church, I hear that there
are divisions among you, and I partly believe it.

19 For there must also be heresies among you so that those who are
approved may be made manifest among you.

20 When you come together therefore in one place, it is not to eat the
Lord's supper.

21 For in eating everyone takes his own supper first, and one is hungry,
and another is drunken.

22 What? Do you not have houses to eat and to drink in? Or do
you disrespect the church of God, and shame those who are
poor? What shall I say to you? Will I commend you in this? I do
not commend you.

The Meaning of Communion

23 For I have received of the Lord that which also I delivered to
you, that the Lord Jesus the same night in which he was betrayed
took bread:

24 and when He had given thanks, He broke it, and said, **"Take,
and eat: this is My body, which is broken for you. Do this in
remembrance of Me" (see Matthew 26:26).**

25 After the supper He also took the cup in the same way, saying,
**"This cup is the new testament in My blood. As often as you
drink it, do this in remembrance of Me" (see Matthew 26:27).**

6 For as often as you eat this bread, and drink this cup, you do declare the Lord's death until He comes.

27 Therefore, whoever eats this bread and drinks this cup of the Lord in an unworthy manner will be guilty of the body and blood of the Lord.

28 Let a man examine himself, and then let him eat of the bread, and drink of the cup.

29 Because he that eats and drinks unworthily, eats and drinks judgment to himself, because he does not discern the Lord's body.

30 For this reason many are weak and sick among you, and some even sleep.

31 If we would judge ourselves we would not have to be judged.

32 When we are judged, we are chastened by the Lord so that we will not be condemned with the world.

33 My brethren, when you come together to eat, wait for one another.

34 If any man is hungry, let him eat at home, so that you do not come under condemnation. The rest will I set in order when I come.

Headship

I Corinthians 11:1-16: Headship is different than just having authority over others. An elder's leadership is not headship. Rather, it is authority in the specific realm of the church fellowship that does not extend over the households or other parts of the lives of members. Headship, however, speaks of being in authority over every part of our lives, a place only Christ has over His people.

This teaching on the head covering was only found in the church at Corinth. There is no other mention of it in any other church in the first century in either the apostles' letters or in history. This was the teaching of the modern church in Corinth because local temple prostitutes were all shorn of their hair. When some of them converted and became part of the church, this head covering for women became a custom in Corinth in order that these former temple prostitutes might not be distinguished as such while their hair grew out, thus protecting them from the shame of their former life.

Whether this is true or not, this custom was limited to the Corinthian church. It was never imposed on other churches. Therefore, it is right that it has not been promoted as a practice for all churches for all time. This is why the apostle completes this exhortation by saying that if any are contentious because of this practice, it is not to be considered a custom of the churches.

A Second Call to Unity

11:17-22: The unity of His people is obviously one of the greatest desires of the Lord. Therefore, to bring division to His people is one of the most injurious things we can do to the Lord Himself, as well as to His people. We are told in Proverbs 6:19 that spreading strife among brothers is one of the seven things the Lord hates. Therefore, one of the basic devotions of every believer should be to never bring strife or division in the church.

The Meaning of Communion

11:23-34: The ritual of communion represents the common-union we have in Christ and His body. To participate in an unworthy manner is to partake of the ritual without having the reality that it represents in our lives. The ritual is simply intended to remind us of our commitment to union with Christ and His people.

One of the most common questions among believers is why Christians get sick and die prematurely. This is the only text in Scripture that addresses this question. There is an automatic judgment of those who partake of the ritual without fulfilling what it represents. That judgment is weakness, sickness, and death. It is not something God does to those who are disobedient. Rather, it is what will surely happen when we are not rightly joined to the Lord and His body. When a member of our natural body gets severed from the body, it will quickly die if not reattached. In the same way, this will happen to believers who get cut off from the body of Christ.

Koinonia

As we are told in I John 1:7, "If we abide in the light as He is in the light, we have fellowship with one another, and the blood of Jesus His Son cleanses us from all sin." The Greek word translated "fellowship" in this text is *koinonia*, the same word that is translated "communion" in this chapter of Corinthians. This word implies a union so great that to break up the union would cause the death of each member. This is a level of union that is rarely found anywhere in the body of Christ. However, as John wrote, this will be found where we are truly abiding in the light. This union is necessary for cleansing by the blood of Jesus, just as the complete union of the members of our body is necessary for our blood to flow through it. Our failure to attain this level of union with the Lord and His body will remain an opening for weakness, sickness, and premature death in the body of Christ.

We cannot be properly joined to the Head without also being properly joined to His body. There are teachings circulating today that say we can have church just by meeting for coffee. In truth, we can have deeper fellowship around coffee than in church services that allow little or no interaction among the people. However, this is still a superficial level of connection. As we proceed toward the end of this age, we must come to know the full meaning of *koinonia* and truly experience it, or we will not survive.

NOTES:

PAUL'S FIRST LETTER TO THE
CORINTHIANS
I Corinthians 12

Spiritual Gifts

1 I would not have you ignorant concerning spiritual gifts, brethren.

2 You know that when you were Gentiles, you were carried away to follow dumb idols, which you were taught to do.

3 Therefore I urge you to understand that no man speaking by the Spirit of God calls Jesus accursed. Likewise, no man can declare that Jesus is the Lord except by the Holy Spirit.

4 Now there are diversities of gifts, but they are from the same Spirit.

5 There are differences of administrations, but they are from the same Lord.

6 There are diversities of operations, but it is the same God that works all in all.

7 The manifestation of the Spirit is given to each one for the profit of all.

8 For to one is given by the Spirit the word of wisdom, and to another the word of knowledge by the same Spirit.

9 To another faith is given by the same Spirit, and to another the gifts of healing by the same Spirit.

10 To another the working of miracles, and to another prophecy. To another discerning of spirits, and to another different kinds of tongues, and to another the interpretation of tongues.

11 All these work through the same Spirit, dividing to every man severally as He will.

The Unity of the Body

12 For as the body is one, and has many members, and all the members of that one body, being many, are one body, so also is Christ.

13 For by one Spirit are we all baptized into one body, whether we are Jews or Gentiles, whether we are bond or free, we have all been made to drink of the one Spirit.

14 For the body is not one member, but many.

15 If the foot shall say, "Because I am not the hand, I am not a part of the body." Is it because of this not a part of the body?

16 If the ear shall say, "Because I am not the eye, I am not a part of the body." Is it not a part of the body?

17 If the whole body was an eye, where would the hearing be? If the whole body was for hearing, where would the smelling be?

18 God has now established each of the members of the body as it has pleased Him.

19 If they were all the same member, how would we be a body?

20 Now they are many members, yet but one body.

21 The eye cannot say to the hand, "I have no need of you." Neither can the hand say to the feet, "I have no need of you."

22 How much more necessary are those members of the body which seem to be more feeble?

23 Those members of the body that we think to be less honorable we bestow more abundant honor. In this way the less attractive parts then become more attractive.

24 For our attractive parts have no need of being given this honor, but God has so fashioned the body together to give more abundant honor to that part which lacked.

25 In this way there should be no division in the body, but that the members should have the same care for one another.

26 When one member suffers, all of the members suffer with it. Or when one member is honored, all of the members rejoice with it.

27 Now you are the body of Christ, as well as individual members in particular.

Order of Ministries

28 God has set some in the church, first apostles, second prophets, third teachers, after that miracles, then gifts of healing, helps, governments, and diversities of tongues.

29 Are all apostles? Are all prophets? Are all teachers? Are all workers of miracles?

30 Do all have the gifts of healing? Do all speak with tongues? Do all interpret?

31 But earnestly desire the best gifts, and yet I will show to you a more excellent way.

Spiritual Gifts

I Corinthians 12:1-11: When Jesus walked the earth, He manifested all of the gifts of the Spirit listed here. When He ascended, He gave these spiritual gifts to His people so that He could continue His ministry through them. As we are told in verse 7, manifestations of the Spirit are given to each one. Every Christian is called to ministry, and every Christian is given a gift, or gifts, of the Spirit as tools for accomplishing their ministry.

Paul also continued to fortify the need for *koinonia* by explaining how the body has many different members but is still one body. No member can say of any other member that they are not needed, regardless of how different they may be. In fact, we must be different from one another. A body with a perfect heart will still die without a set of lungs, and one with perfect eyes will not fare very well without arms and legs.

The Unity of the Body

12:12-27: Because each of us has been given different aspects of the ministry Christ walked in, we do not fully manifest His ministry unless we walk together in unity, each one manifesting their uniqueness. This is a unity of diversity, not conformity. Presently, most churches divide into congregations or movements, contrary to this wisdom. Evangelists tend to gather in one group, teachers in another, prophetic people

in another, etc., which causes imbalances and divisions in the body. In order to be complete, we need the different parts of the body working together and walking together in unity.

Order of Ministries

12:28-31: The order in which these ministries are set in the church reflects the order in which their impartation is needed to build the church. Laying the foundation is the role of apostles and prophets. Then there is the need for teachers to bring understanding and then the miracle ministries.

It is interesting that the ministry of helps is listed before governments. We often think of the ministry of helps as attending to menial tasks, but that is only one aspect of this ministry. Helps is the basis of all ministry, which is the manifestation of the Holy Spirit, who is the Helper. The ministry of helps is supernaturally empowered, but it is also the nature of helping that will be inclined to engage in every task that needs to be done.

SPECIAL NOTE: The Corinthian church is often referred to as "the carnal church" because of the rebukes in these letters for their carnal behavior. This was especially due to divisions, but even adultery was tolerated with seemingly no one to challenge it. Dispensationalists who do not believe in the present operation of the gifts of the Spirit blame this carnality on their pursuit of the gifts. Contrary to their mentality, Paul, who has already rebuked them for their carnality, then encourages the pursuit of spiritual gifts, which is a very obvious remedy for the carnality, not a cause of it.

The warnings in Scripture for blaming the Holy Spirit for such things as carnality are most severe. We should be careful not to entertain such foolishness. On the contrary, we should accept the biblical exhortations to seek spiritual gifts. These are tools that are essential for the building up of the body of Christ, which is to represent Him by becoming like Him and doing the works that He did. Even so, being entrusted with the greatest gifts does not give us license to follow the lusts of our flesh. Scripture clearly states, "those who practice such things will not inherit the kingdom of God" (see Galatians 5). Even if we have the greatest power gifts of the Spirit, we are not exempted from walking in the fruit of the Spirit.

NOTES:

Paul's First Letter To The
CORINTHIANS
I Corinthians 13

The Greatest of All

1 Though I speak with the tongues of men and of angels, but do not have love, I have become like a sounding brass, or a tinkling cymbal.

2 Though I have the gift of prophecy, and understand all mysteries, and all knowledge, and though I have all faith so that I could remove mountains, if I do not have love, I am nothing.

3 Though I give all my possessions to feed the poor, and though I give my body to be burned, if I do not have love, it profits me nothing.

4 Love is patient; love is kind. Love does not envy. Love does not promote itself, and is not arrogant.

5 Love does not behave in an unseemly manner. It does not seek its own, is not easily provoked, and does not have evil thoughts.

6 Love does not rejoice in iniquity, but rejoices in the truth.

7 Love bears all things, believes all things, hopes all things, endures all things.

Ultimate Success

8 Love never fails, but prophecy will cease, as will tongues, and even knowledge will come to an end.

9 For we know in part, and we prophesy in part,

10 so when that which is perfect has come, then that which is in part will be done away with.

11 When I was a child, I spoke as a child, I understood as a child, and I thought as a child, but when I became a man I put away childish things.

12 For now we see through a glass darkly, but then we will see face to face. Now I know in part, but then I will know even just as I am known.

13 These three: faith, hope, and love, will abide, but the greatest of these is love.

The Greatest of All

I Corinthians 13:1-7: To the degree that we love, we achieve the greatest honor recognized for eternity. Our highest goal and greatest achievement is love. The greatest human being is the one who loves the most—first God, then one another. Such a life will be a marvel and capture the attention of the world, just as Mother Teresa remains a great modern example. Such a person would also be the happiest of all people on earth, filled with the joy that is normal Christianity.

Ultimate Success

13:8-13: The means for guaranteed success without a possibility of failure is this: "Love never fails." What we do in love will never be a failure.

This could also be translated, "Love never quits." Those who know the truth and seek to live it will be strong in life, but not as strong as those who love truth. Scripture tells us that those who love truth will not be deceived. Just having truth will not keep us from deception; only those motivated by love will never quit or be deceived.

Verse 10 is often given to justify the doctrine that the gifts of the Spirit are no longer functioning in the church today. Such people believe "that which is perfect" is The Bible, and once it came, the gifts were no longer needed. If that were true, then as this verse states, knowledge would be done away with also. Obviously it has not—neither has prophecy, nor the other gifts. Basing such an important doctrine on a single verse (not to mention using an interpretation that is so ambiguous) violates the most basic principles of exegesis and has led to this false and destructive doctrine.

Even though this doctrine, which would negate much of the work of the Holy Spirit in the church, may be foolish and biblically baseless, a primary, if unstated, reason many reject the present operation of the gifts of the Spirit is because those who walk in them seem to be lacking in the character and fruit of the Holy Spirit. As this chapter also makes clear, the greatest gifts and the greatest faith mean nothing if we do not have love. If we want to live a life that cannot fail, then we must pursue love above all things. However, that does not mean we stop pursuing the gifts of the Spirit. We pursue the gifts of the Spirit because Scripture commands us to do so and because we love people and want to be used by the Holy Spirit to help them.

NOTES:

PAUL'S FIRST LETTER TO THE
CORINTHIANS
I Corinthians 14

Pursuing Love by Pursuing Spiritual Gifts

1 Pursue love and desire spiritual gifts, especially that you may prophesy.

2 Because he that speaks in an unknown tongue does not speak to men, but to God. So no man can understand him for he is speaking mysteries in the Spirit.

3 He that prophesies speaks to men for their edification, and exhortation, and comfort.

4 He that speaks in an unknown tongue edifies himself, but he that prophesies edifies the church.

5 I would have you all to speak with tongues, but even more so that you would prophesy. Greater is he that prophesies than he that speaks with tongues, unless they interpret so that the church may be edified.

6 If I come to you speaking with tongues, what will I profit you unless I speak to you either by revelation, or knowledge, or prophecy, or teaching?

7 Even things without life that give a sound, such as a pipe or harp, unless they give a distinct sound how will it be known what is played?

8 If the trumpet gives an uncertain sound, who will prepare himself for battle?

9 It is the same with you. Unless you speak in words easy to be understood, how can it be known what you are saying? Otherwise it is as if you are just speaking into the air.

10 There are many different languages in the world, and none of them are without importance.

11 If I do not know the meaning of the language, I will be to him that speaks a barbarian, and he that speaks will be like a barbarian to me.

12 Even so, as much as you are zealous for spiritual gifts, seek that you may excel to the edifying of the church.

13 Therefore let him that speaks in an unknown tongue pray that he may interpret.

14 For if I pray in an unknown tongue my spirit prays, but I have not gained any understanding.

15 What is our conclusion then? I will pray with the Spirit, and I will pray with my understanding also. I will sing with the Spirit, and I will sing with my understanding also.

16 Otherwise, when you will bless with the Spirit, how will he that occupies the place of the unlearned say "Amen" at your giving of thanks, seeing that he does not understand what you are saying?

17 For you to give thanks is good, but the other is not edified.

18 I thank my God that I speak with tongues more than all of you,

19 yet in the church I would rather speak five words with my understanding than ten thousand words in an unknown tongue, so that I might teach others also.

20 Brethren, do not be immature in your understanding. In malice be as children, but in understanding be men.

21 In the law it is written, "**With men of other tongues and other lips will I speak to this people and yet they still will not hear Me,' says the Lord" (Isaiah 28:11,12).**

22 Therefore, tongues are for a sign, not to those who believe, but to those who do not believe. However, prophesying is for those who believe.

23 If therefore the whole church is together in one place, and all speak with tongues, and those come in who do not understand what you are doing, or are unbelievers, will they not say that you are insane?

24 But if all prophesy, and one comes in that does not believe, or has not been taught in spiritual things, he will still be convinced by all, and convicted by all,

25 as the secrets of his heart are disclosed so that he will fall on his face and worship God, declaring that God is certainly among you.

26 How is it then brethren, that when you come together, every one of you has a psalm, a teaching, a tongue, a revelation, an interpretation? Let all things be done for edification.

27 If any man speaks in an unknown tongue, let it be by two, or at the most by three, and then let one interpret.

28 If there is no interpreter, let him keep silent in the church, and let him speak to himself, and to God.

29 Let the prophets speak two or three at a time, and let the others judge.

30 If anything is revealed to another that sits by, let the first hold his peace.

31 For you may all prophesy one by one so that all may learn, and all may be comforted.

32 Remember that the spirits of the prophets are subject to the prophets.

33 Our God is not the author of confusion, but of peace, as in all churches of the saints.

The Place of Women in the Church

34 You say, "Let the women keep silent in the churches, for it is not permitted for them to speak, but they are commanded to be under obedience, as the Law also says.

35 If they will learn anything, let them ask their husbands at home, for it is a shame for women to speak in the church."

36 What? Did the word of God come only to you?

37 If any man thinks of himself as a prophet, or spiritual, let him acknowledge that the things I write to you are the commandments of the Lord.

38 If any man is ignorant, let him be ignorant.

39 Therefore, brethren, covet the ability to prophesy, but do not forbid to speak with tongues.

40 Let all things be done decently and in order.

Pursuing Love by Pursuing Spiritual Gifts

I Corinthians 14:1-33: The last verse before Chapter Thirteen is about pursuing the gifts of the Spirit. Then the chapter that follows is about seeking and using the gifts of the Spirit. Again, to pursue love does not mean we do not pursue the gifts of the Spirit, but we pursue them as a way to express the love of God. If we do this, it will always edify the church.

We are told to especially pursue the gift of prophecy. Prophecy is communication and guidance from God, which is the most valuable gift we can be given. Communication is the basis of every relationship, including our relationship with God. The quality of any relationship will be based on the quality of the communication. Prophecy is a primary way that God has always communicated with His people. Scripture tells us that Enoch was the first to walk with God after Adam, and it says that he "prophesied." A good case can be made that everyone who walks with God will prophesy or be one through whom God will speak.

For those who say that God no longer speaks through prophecy because we now have The Bible through which He speaks, we should ask: How would you feel on your wedding day if your spouse came up to you and said, "I wrote this book for you so that I will never have to speak to you again"? We are told that man does not live by bread alone but by every word that proceeds from the mouth of God—present tense, not that proceeded, past tense. Our relationship with God is meant to be a living, present one, and this relationship requires present communication. Prophecy has been a primary means by which the Lord communicates with His people, since the time of Enoch to today.

Even so, prophecy is never used for establishing doctrine. The Bible alone is for establishing doctrine. The Bible also preserves the record of God's dealings with men so that we can understand His ways. Much of The Bible is also devoted to prophecy. However, The Bible was never intended to displace the living communication between God and His people. Neither is prophecy intended to take the place of The Bible as the source of doctrine. Those who have claimed prophetic words that establish doctrine have become cults and sects full of deception. Anyone who attempts to use prophecy to change or establish doctrine is misusing it. Prophecy is meant to reveal the strategic and tactical will of God, as well as to simply communicate with and relate to His people.

The Place of Women in the Church

14:34-40: There are sections of Paul's letters that are believed to be quotes of the questions sent to him from the church he was writing to. Paul then answers these questions, which many theologians agree was the case here. It could not have been Paul's teaching that women were to keep silent in the church for a number of reasons:

Paul gives instructions that if women prophesied, let them do so with their heads covered. How could they prophesy if they could not speak?

It is stated here that "the Law" also says that women should keep silent. Nowhere does the Law say this, and Paul, a former "Pharisee of Pharisees," a sect that required the memorization of Torah, would certainly have known this.

Paul practiced esteeming the teaching of women, as he did with Priscilla, who he commended for giving instructions to one of the foremost teachers of the first century, Apollos.

It is a basic theological principle that if one verse stands out in opposition to the entire weight of Scripture, we must not base our doctrine on the one verse, but rather on the weight of Scripture. The entire weight of Scripture is that God has placed no limitations on anyone who seeks Him, male or female, old or young, tribe or race.

NOTES:

Paul's First Letter To The
CORINTHIANS
I Corinthians 15

The Gospel Truth

1 Even so, brethren, I declare to you the gospel that I preached to you, that you have received, upon which you stand,

2 and by which you are saved, if you remember what I preached to you, unless you have believed in vain.

3 For I delivered to you first of all that which I also received, how that Christ died for our sins just as the Scriptures foretold.

4 He was buried, and He rose again the third day according to the Scriptures.

The Apostolic Witnesses

5 He was seen by Cephas, then by the twelve,

6 and after that He was seen by more than five hundred brethren at once, of whom the greater part remain to this present time, but some have fallen asleep.

7 Then He was seen by James; then by all of the apostles.

8 Last of all He was seen by me, as to one untimely born.

9 For I am the least of the apostles, and am not worthy to be called an apostle, because I persecuted the church of God.

10 It is by the grace of God I am what I am, and His grace which was bestowed upon me was not in vain. I labored more abundantly than all of them, yet not I, but the grace of God that was with me.

11 Therefore whether it were I, or they, so we preached, and so you believed.

The Resurrection

12 If it is preached that Christ rose from the dead, how do some of you say that there is no resurrection of the dead?

13 If there is no resurrection of the dead then Christ has not risen.

14 If Christ has not risen then our preaching is in vain, and your faith is also in vain.

15 Yes, and we are then false witnesses of God, because we have testified that God raised up Christ, whom He did not raise up if it is so that the dead are not raised.

16 For if the dead do not rise, then Christ is not raised either,

17 and if Christ is not raised, your faith is vain; you are yet in your sins.

18 Then those who have fallen asleep in Christ have perished.

19 If it is in this life only that we have hope in Christ, we are of all men the most miserable.

20 However, Christ has risen from the dead, and become the first fruits of those that sleep.

21 For since by a man came death, by a man also came the resurrection from the dead.

22 Just as in Adam all die, even so in Christ will all be made alive.

23 Every man in his own order: Christ, the first fruits, and after that those who are Christ's at His coming.

The Kingdom Coming

24 Then the end will come when He will have delivered up the kingdom to God the Father, after He will have put down all rule, and all authority, and power.

25 For He must reign until He has put all of His enemies under His feet.

26 The last enemy that will be destroyed is death.

27 Because He has put all things under His feet, when He says all things are put under Him, it is obvious that He is excepted who put all things under Him.

28 When all things are subdued by Him, then the Son will also Himself be subject to Him that put all things under Him, that God may be all in all.

29 Otherwise, why are those baptized for the dead, if the dead do not rise?

Apostolic Sacrifice

30 So why do we risk ourselves every hour?

31 I protest! It is because of the joy that I have in you being in Christ Jesus our Lord that I die daily.

32 If it was for the favor of men that I have fought with beasts at Ephesus, what benefit is this to me? If the dead do not rise let us eat and drink, for tomorrow we die.

33 Do not be deceived—bad company corrupts good morals.

34 Awake to righteousness, and do not sin, for some do not have the knowledge of God. I speak this to your shame.

The Resurrected Body

35 Some will say, "How are the dead raised up? What body will they have?"

36 You foolish man! That which you sow is not quickened unless it first dies.

37 That which you sow is not the body that it will be, but a mere grain, whether it is wheat, or some other grain.

38 God gives it a body as it has pleased Him, and to every seed its own body.

39 All flesh is not the same. There is one kind of flesh for men, another for beasts, another for fish, and another for birds.

40 There are also celestial bodies and terrestrial bodies. The glory of the celestial is one, and the glory of the terrestrial is different.

41 There is one glory of the sun, another glory of the moon, another glory of the stars, and then each star differs from another star in glory.

42 So also is the resurrection of the dead. The body is sown in a corruptible state, but it is raised in incorruption.

43 It is sown in dishonor, but it is raised in glory. It is sown in weakness, but it is raised in power.

44 It is sown a natural body, but it is raised a spiritual body. There is a natural body, and there is a spiritual body.

45 For this reason it is written, "The first man Adam was made a living soul; the last Adam was made a quickening spirit."

46 However, it is not the spiritual that is first, but that which is natural, and afterward that which is spiritual.

47 The first man is of the earth, earthly; the second man is the Lord from heaven.

48 As is the earthly, such are they also that are earthly. As is the heavenly, such are they also that are heavenly.

49 Just as we have borne the image of the earthly, we will also bear the image of the heavenly.

The Great Transformation

50 Now this I say, brethren, that flesh and blood cannot inherit the kingdom of God, and neither does corruption inherit incorruption.

51 Behold, I will tell you a mystery: we will not all sleep, but we will all be changed.

52 In a moment, in the twinkling of an eye, at the last trumpet. For the trumpet will sound, and the dead will be raised incorruptible, and we will be changed.

53 For the corruptible must put on incorruption, and the mortal must put on immortality.

54 So when this corruptible body will have put on incorruption, and this mortal body will have put on immortality, then it will have come to pass that which was written, **"Death is swallowed up in victory"** (see Isaiah 25:8).

55 **"O death, where is your sting? O grave, where is your victory?" (see Hosea 13:14)**

56 The sting of death is sin, and the power of sin is the Law.

57 Thanks be to God, who gives us the victory through our Lord Jesus Christ.

58 Therefore, my beloved brethren, be steadfast, unmovable, always abounding in the work of the Lord, knowing that your labor is not in vain in the Lord.

The Gospel Truth

I Corinthians 15:1-4: There will never be a greater testimony of the love of God than how Christ died for our sins. There will never be a greater testimony of the power of His love than "He rose again from the dead." Because of this, we have assurance that we too will rise again. Death will not be our end, it will be a new beginning more glorious than we can imagine.

I was once deeply challenged when a nurse asked, "Why don't Christians die better?" She had a point. Every Christian should die laughing with great joy. Death is the end of all suffering and the beginning of unimaginable joy. This is the truth upon which we stand. It is the strongest foundation one can ever stand on and compels us to live the way we should live—ever willing to sacrifice for the purposes of the Lord and to serve others, knowing we will have our reward for eternity.

The Apostolic Witnesses

15:5-11: One of the qualifications for being an apostle is to have seen the resurrected Christ. This is because Christ and the resurrection are the apostolic message. When we return to these most powerful and encompassing of all truths, we too will see apostolic results.

The Resurrection

15:12-23: Resurrection is the most important benefit of the New Covenant. It is by living for the resurrection that our present life takes on its true meaning—"training for reigning" for the age to come and qualifying as joint heirs with Christ in the family of God. Every other New Covenant truth is based upon the truth of the resurrection—death has been defeated. This is why the resurrection remains the main focus of distortion and corruption by the enemy. When we believe in the resurrection in our hearts and not just as a doctrine, we will live free of the fear of death, which is the greatest freedom we can know and the greatest witness of the truth.

The Kingdom Coming

15:24-29: It will take some time to subdue all the enemies of the Lord after His kingdom has been established. His physical reign on earth will be a thousand years, because it will be a process of renewal and restoration. Even though Satan will be bound and all will know that Jesus is Lord, life will be easier; however, it will still take time to restore mankind and the earth. To take time and do His work with great patience and depth has been the way of the Lord from the beginning, just as He has patiently worked with each of us.

Apostolic Sacrifice

15:30-34: This teaching is intended to compel the Corinthians to serve the Lord in all things and grow to maturity in Him. Paul explained that for the sake of the Lord's purpose for them, he was willing to lay down his life every day.

The Resurrected Body

15:35-49: Jesus did not come to show us how God lives, but how we are to live. His resurrection is also a model of our resurrection. His resurrected body manifested in the flesh and still carried the scars of His crucifixion, but was also Spirit so that He could pass through walls or manifest anywhere at any time. The resurrected body is obviously not subject to natural laws and has the power to manifest in the flesh, but it is also spiritual and incorruptible.

The Lord also told His disciples immediately after His resurrection that He had not yet been "glorified." As Paul witnessed on the road to Damascus, His glorified body is brighter than the sun. Yet the Book of Acts records later appearances of the Lord, such as when He stood before Paul to tell him he would appear in Rome, in which He obviously did not stand in His blinding glory (see Acts 23:11).

The Great Transformation

15:50-58: This weak and frail body will be exchanged for an incorruptible one. This will happen in "the twinkling of an eye." This is the victory over death, and ultimately all death will be defeated. As Paul summed up in the last verse, this is why we labor, and this labor will not be in vain. The victory is sure!

In this discourse the apostle states, "the power of sin is the Law." The Law was not given to promote sin or empower it, but when the Law is wrongly used as legalism, that is the result. The Law was given as a tutor to lead us to Christ. It was meant to manifest our sin so that we would know its power, but also so that we would turn to the only remedy for sin—the atonement of the cross. When we do not turn to the cross but seek to resolve our sinful nature with legalism, it empowers the sin and will never lead to freedom from sin.

NOTES:

PAUL'S FIRST LETTER TO THE
CORINTHIANS
1 Corinthians 16

Offerings

1   Now concerning the collection for the saints, as I have given order to the churches of Galatia, you should do the same.

2   On the first day of the week let every one of you contribute as God has prospered him, so that there does not have to be collections when I come.

3   When I come, whom you approve will go with your letters to bring your generous gift to Jerusalem.

4   If it is right for me to go, they will go with me.

Paul's Itinerary

5   I will come to you when I pass through Macedonia.

6   It may be that I will stay with you for the winter, so that you can help send me on my journey wherever I go from there.

7   For I do not want to just see you in passing, but will come when I can stay with you for a while, if the Lord permits.

8   However, I will tarry at Ephesus until Pentecost,

9   because a great door for effectual service has opened to me there, and there are many adversaries.

Commending Fellow Workers

10 Now if Timothy comes, see that he may dwell with you without fear, for he does the work of the Lord as I also do.

11 Do not let any man despise him, but send him forth in peace so that he may come to me, for I look for him with the brethren.

12 As for our brother Apollos, I greatly desired for him to go to you with the brethren, but it was not his will to do so at this time, but he will come when it is more convenient.

13 Watch yourselves, stand fast in the faith, stand like men, be strong.

14 Let all things be done in love.

15 As you know the house of Stephen, that they were the first fruits of Achaia, how they have a great devotion to the ministry of the saints,

16 I beseech you to submit yourselves to such as them, and to everyone that helps with us, and labors.

17 I am glad for the coming of Stephen, and Fortunatus, and Achaicus: because that which was left undone on your part they have supplied.

18 For they have refreshed my spirit and yours. Therefore acknowledge those who are like them.

19 The churches of Asia salute you. Aquila and Priscilla salute you in the Lord, along with the church that is in their house.

20 All the brethren greet you. Greet one another with a holy kiss.

21 The salutation is from me, Paul, with my own hand.

22 If any man does not love the Lord Jesus Christ, let him be accursed. Maranatha.

23 The grace of our Lord Jesus Christ be with you.

24 My love is with you all in Christ Jesus. Amen.

Offerings

I Corinthians 16:1-4: As is apparent here, and in other writings of the early church fathers, New Testament churches held to the commandment of giving the first fruits to the Lord for the service of His house, the church. These first fruits were given on the first day of the week and used to support those who needed to get their sustenance from the gospel, or they were distributed to the needy in the body of Christ. As we read in other places in the New Testament, it was considered right for the church to share its natural blessings with those who were responsible for their spiritual blessings—the Jewish people, which took precedence in their support of needy brethren.

Paul's Itinerary

16:5-9: Paul indicates that one way he knew that a great door for effective service had been opened to him was because there were many adversaries. This is quite a contrast to the mentality of many today who seem to believe that something is from the Lord if it comes easy for them. The true biblical principle is that anything that comes too easy or too fast is usually insignificant.

Commending Fellow Workers

16:10-24: Paul knew well those who labored in truth for the Lord, and he gave them his endorsement with these recommendations. There were already many false apostles who had perverted the sound doctrine of the New Covenant. Therefore, these recommendations carried a lot of weight with the churches. The ones whom Paul recommended were not only sound in doctrine, but they were also impeccable in character and devotion to the Lord. We should always seek to maintain such standards for those allowed to minister in the household of God. Those who maintain this integrity throughout their course are the crown jewels of the church age.

Paul's first letter to the Corinthians is no doubt one of the most important in the New Testament for illuminating the functioning of the New Covenant church and for showing how problems and disputes were judged and resolved. Some loose ends remain in this epistle, but they are wonderfully resolved in Paul's second letter to the Corinthians.

NOTES:

Paul's First Letter to the Corinthians Proper Names and Meanings

Achaia: grief, trouble

Achaicus: from Achaia, sorrowing, sad

Aquila: an eagle

Asia: muddy, boggy

Apollos: one who destroys, destroyer

Barnabas: son of consolation, son of encouragement

Cephas: a stone

Chloe: green herb

Christ: anointed

Corinth: which is satisfied, ornament, beauty

Crispus: curled

Ephesus: desirable

Fortunatus: lucky, fortunate

Gaius: lord, an earthly man

Galatia: white, the color of milk

Gentiles: the nations, or pagan

Israel: who prevails with God, a prince with God

James: one who supplants undermines,

Jerusalem: city of peace, vision of peace, foundation of peace, restoring or teaching of peace

Jesus: savior, deliverer, Yahweh is salvation

Jew: the praise of the Lord, (derived from Judah)

Job: he that weeps or cries, he who turns

Macedonia: burning, adoration

Maranatha: the Lord is coming

Moses: taken out, drawn forth

Passover: to pass or to spring over, to spare

Pentecost: fiftieth

Priscilla: ancient

Paul: small, little

Satan: contrary, adversary, enemy, accuser, deceiver

Sosthenes: savior, strong, powerful

Stephen: crown, crowned

PAUL'S SECOND LETTER TO THE
CORINTHIANS

This letter is believed to have been written within months of Paul's first letter to the Corinthians, probably around 56 AD. The reason for this is the apparent closeness of events addressed in both letters. Like the first letter, this epistle is also a remarkable example of the pastoral heart of the great apostle.

As we saw in the first letter, the Corinthian church, in which Paul had labored much to see it planted and growing, had become embroiled in deep divisions and other major problems. His recent visit to them had obviously not gone well. In the first letter, he had been more confrontational and challenging than in any of his other writings. He knew that if they did not receive his message as intended, his relationship with that important church might be permanently damaged. Then he received word that the church had not only taken his rebukes very well, with repentance and tears, but they had expressed great love and appreciation for their spiritual father. Paul's joy was like that of a father who had been reconciled to his children. This second letter was quickly written to them in response.

As is typical with all of Paul's letters, this one was Christ-centered and strong in fortifying the basics of the faith. Paul offered insights into reasons why we suffer. At the same time, he shared his own feelings and struggles, which he related in a way to encourage the Corinthians to face hardships as opportunities to grow in the Lord. As was also his habit, Paul completed his teachings and exhortations with hope for the future and for the continued spreading of the gospel. Paul obviously defined the success of his life and ministry by the spreading of the gospel and the maturing of those who embraced it who would continue to grow in Christ.

Paul went on to explain that the evidence of the church's maturity was their generosity. This was addressed in Chapter Nine in one of the greatest of all discourses on this subject. All who are maturing in Christ will grow in generosity. The basis of the gospel is that the Father loved us so much that He gave His best—His own Son. Therefore, all who are growing in His nature will be increasingly generous givers. This will result in more of the grace of God until "all grace" abounds in our lives, which results in being trusted with even more to give.

Along with this devotion to generosity, which Paul exhorted all to have, he was also concerned that these generous gifts be properly managed in order to give no occasion for reproach on this ministry. Only the most trustworthy saints were allowed to accompany the apostles for transporting and disbursing the gifts. This proved to be prophetic, as did virtually all of Paul's teachings. Throughout the church age, one of the greatest reproaches against the church and the gospel has come from the mishandling of the resources entrusted to it. It is right to teach the saints generosity, but it is also crucial to teach integrity and good management with all that is given.

Paul then gave an insightful exhortation on apostolic authority when he defended his own apostleship. It may be surprising that he does not recount how many people he has led to the Lord, or how many churches he established to verify his apostolic ministry. Instead, he recounted his persecutions and afflictions.

Paul understood well the principle that spiritual authority is released through the cross; through suffering for the sake of the gospel. Just as Scripture says that we are healed by the stripes that Jesus took, the same is true for us. In the very place where we are wounded, we can receive authority for healing others. Suffering for the gospel is not only one of the great honors that we can have in this life, but it is a basis for the authority we can be entrusted with. Paul had been wounded often for the gospel, and the authority he carried was so great that his letters would become canon Scripture. He is still probably bearing more fruit for eternal life through them than possibly all of the ministries laboring today.

We also see through this letter the depth to which Paul remained concerned for the well-being of those he had led to Christ, like a true parent. When they fell into sin, he grieved. When they did well, he rejoiced. He did not merely include them in a membership number, but he kept them in his heart. He prayed for them and continued to speak into their lives. Paul did not just make converts, but he made disciples as The Great Commission demanded.

Paul also spoke of great revelations he had received, but then he reverted right back to describing his own weaknesses. Paul knew well and lived by the truth that God's strength is made perfect in weakness. He did his best to help the Corinthians understand this, so they would not continue to trust in carnal strength or external appearances, which are the same pitfalls in the church today that have weakened the body of Christ and have hindered its message since.

Paul's Second Letter To The
CORINTHIANS
II Corinthians 1

Salutation and Comfort for the Afflicted

1 Paul, an apostle of Christ Jesus by the will of God, and Timothy our brother, to the church of God that is at Corinth, and all the saints who are in the whole of Achaia:

2 Grace to you and peace from God our Father and the Lord Jesus Christ.

3 Blessed be the God and Father of our Lord Jesus Christ, the Father of mercies, and the God of all comfort,

4 who comforts us in all of our affliction so that we may be able to comfort those who are in any affliction through the comfort by which we ourselves have been comforted by God.

5 For as our sufferings in Christ are abundant even so our comfort also abounds through Christ.

6 If we are afflicted, it is for your comfort and salvation. If we are comforted, it is also for your comfort that works in you the patient enduring of the same sufferings that we also suffer.

7 Our hope for you is steadfast, knowing that just as you are partakers of the sufferings, so also are you *partakers* of the comfort.

Apostolic Trials

8 For we would not have you ignorant, brethren, concerning our affliction that befell us in Asia. We were burdened exceedingly beyond our own strength, to the degree that we despaired even of life.

9 We had the sentence of death within ourselves so that we would not trust in ourselves, but in God who raises the dead.

10 He delivered us out of so great a death, and will continue to deliver us. It is on Him that we have set our hope, knowing that He will always deliver us.

11 You also help on our behalf by your intercession, so that for the gift bestowed upon us by means of the many, thanks may be given by many persons on our behalf.

12 For our glorifying is this, the testimony of our conscience, that in holiness and sincerity toward God, not in fleshly wisdom, but in the grace of God we behaved ourselves in the world, and more abundantly toward you.

13 For we write only those things to you that you can read and understand, and I hope that you will keep the knowledge of them to the end,

14 just as also you did acknowledge us in part, that we are your glorying, even as you also are ours in the day of our Lord Jesus.

15 In this confidence I was hoping to come to you, that you might have a second benefit,

16 and by you to pass into Macedonia, and again from Macedonia to come to you, and then by you to be sent ahead on my journey to Judea.

The Firm Foundation

17 When I was therefore intending to come, but could not, was I wavering? Or the things that I purpose, do I purpose according to the flesh so that with me there should be both "yes, yes," and the "no, no?"

18 As God is faithful our word toward you is not "yes and no."

19 For the Son of God, Jesus Christ, who was preached among you by us, even by me and Silvanus and Timothy, was not "yes and no," but in Him it is "yes."

20 For as many as the promises of God are, in Him they are "yes." Therefore, also through Him is the "Amen" to the glory of God through us.

21 Now He that establishes us with you in Christ, and anointed us, is God,

22 who also sealed us, and gave us the seal of His ownership, the Spirit in our hearts.

23 I call God for a witness upon my soul that to spare you I did not come to Corinth.

24 Not that we have lordship over your faith, but are co-laborers with you, and this we do with joy, because in your faith you stand fast.

Salutation and Comfort for the Afflicted

II Corinthians 1:1-7: Paul contended that the Corinthian Christians could comfort others with the same comfort by which they had been comforted during their afflictions. The same is true for us. The Lord does not allow the afflictions that come upon us for nothing. He wants to draw us ever closer to the Comforter and to enable us to help others who are going through similar afflictions. One of the best ways to rise out of the depression or discouragement of our own afflictions is to help someone else. To focus on others in the midst of our own suffering takes special grace and faith, and faith pleases God. Faith is the most powerful force on the earth, and faith will lead to our deliverance.

Apostolic Trials

1:8-16: Paul gloried that he kept a right spirit during his afflictions. We too must have a vision for enduring our trials with patience. There is great satisfaction in accomplishing a great project, but there is also great satisfaction in victoriously enduring a test of our faith. Discouragement is a lack of faith, but courage is faith. Be strong and courageous in all things, and your faith will make you whole.

If we determined to do this in everything, we would likely be delivered from trials sooner. If they do not work out sooner, then the benefit of growing our faith is even greater. Even in this, "all things work together for our good." All things that are allowed are intended to work Christlikeness in our lives. By embracing the work of God in us through trials, we can

conform to His likeness much faster and thereby pass through the trials faster, as well as gain more from them.

The Firm Foundation

1:17-24: As Paul said in verse 20, all the promises of God are in Christ, and they are attained by abiding in Him. Therefore, the answer to every trial is to turn to Him, get closer to Him, and abide in Him. He has already overcome the world. Jesus Christ is the answer to every human problem. He does not just have the answer—He is the answer. Let all things do their work to conform you to His image.

NOTES:

Paul's Second Letter To The
CORINTHIANS
II Corinthians 2

Fatherly Sorrow and Compassion

1 I determined for myself that I would not come again to you with sorrow.

2 For if I make you sorry who then is he that gives me joy but he that was made sorry by me?

3 I wrote this very thing so that when I came I would not have sorrow from the very ones in whom I should rejoice, having confidence in you all so that my joy is the same joy as yours.

4 It was out of much affliction and anguish of heart that I wrote to you with many tears, not desiring for you to be made sorry, but that you might know the love that I have even more abundantly for you.

5 Even so, if any have caused sorrow he has not just caused sorrow to me, but in part to all of you, though I would not carry it too far.

6 Sufficient for such a one is this punishment that was carried out by the congregation.

7 Now you should rather forgive him and comfort him, so that he will not be overwhelmed with excessive sorrow.

8 Therefore I beseech you to confirm him and express your love toward him.

9 For to this end also did I write that I might test you to see whether you are obedient in all things.

10 But to whom you forgive anything, I forgive also. What I also have forgiven, if I have forgiven anything, it is for your sakes, and I have done it in the presence of Christ,

11 so that Satan may take no advantage of us, for we are not ignorant of his schemes.

Always Victorious

12 Now when I came to Troas for the gospel of Christ, and when a door was opened to me by the Lord,

13 I had a constant burden in my spirit because I did not find Titus my brother. So, taking my leave of them, I went into Macedonia

14 Thanks be to God, who always leads us in His triumph in Christ, and manifests through us the fragrance of the knowledge of Him in every place.

15 For we are a sweet aroma of Christ to God for those who are saved, and to those that perish.

16 To the one a savor from death to death, but to the other a savor from life to life. Who is sufficient for these things?

17 For we are not as the many, adulterating the Word of God, but in sincerity before God, and in the sight of God, speak we in Christ.

Fatherly Sorrow and Compassion

II Corinthians 2:1-11: Bible scholars assume that this discourse is in reference to the brother that Paul addressed in his first letter to the Corinthians who was boasting about committing adultery with his father's wife (obviously his stepmother). Paul had chastised the church for having not put him out for such a grievous sin. However, here Paul revealed amazing grace and compassion toward the offending brother.

Paul was a hard, intense, focused leader. He had to be in order to accomplish all that he did. Even so, here we see the remarkable love that remained the foundation of his drive. It is love, not legalism that compels sinners to repent. However, God's love never compromises biblical standards of truth, righteousness, and justice so that there can be true repentance and reconciliation with God and those offended by sin.

Always Victorious

2:12-17: Here is another example of Paul's great love. In this case, it was for his disciple and co-worker, Titus. Duty, obliga-

tion, and even the fear of punishment can be motivating forces in our lives. Yet the greatest and most powerful of all motivations is love. Paul labored more than any because he loved so much. He loved so much because he had received the amazing grace of God even when he was persecuting His church. Those who are forgiven much, love much, and a person in love will be the most motivated of all.

NOTES:

PAUL'S SECOND LETTER TO THE
CORINTHIANS
II Corinthians 3

You are God's Letter to the World

1 Are we beginning to commend ourselves again? Or do we need, as do some, letters of commendation to you, or from you?

2 You are our letter, written in our hearts, known and read by all men.

3 It has been made manifest that you are a letter from Christ, ministered to by us, not written with ink, but with the Spirit of the living God, not on tablets of stone, but on the tablets of the hearts of men.

4 Such confidence we have through Christ toward God.

The Greater Glory of the New Covenant

5 Not that we are sufficient in ourselves, or account anything as being from ourselves, but our sufficiency is from God,

6 who also made us sufficient as ministers of a new covenant, not of the letter, but of the Spirit, because the letter kills, but the Spirit gives life.

7 So if the administration of death, written and engraved on stones, came with glory, so that the children of Israel could not look steadfastly upon the face of Moses because of the glory of his face, fading away as it was,

8 shall not the administration of the Spirit be with even more glory?

9 If the administration of condemnation has glory, much more does the administration of righteousness exceed it in glory.

10 Obviously, that which has been glorious now has less glory because of the glory that surpasses it.

11 For if that which passes away was with glory, much more will that which remains be in glory.

12 Having therefore such a hope we use great boldness of speech,

13 and are not as Moses who put a veil upon his face so that the children of Israel could not look steadfastly on that which was passing away.

14 Their minds were hardened, and until this very day at the reading of the Old Covenant the same veil remains, it not being revealed to them that it is done away with in Christ.

15 To this day whenever Moses is read a veil lies over their heart.

The Glory that Changes Us

16 Even so, whenever one turns to the Lord, the veil is taken away.

17 Now the Lord is the Spirit, and where the Spirit of the Lord is there is liberty.

18 We all, with an unveiled face, beholding as in a mirror the glory of the Lord, are being transformed into the same image from glory to glory, even as from the Spirit of the Lord.

You are God's Letter to the World

II Corinthians 3:1-4: Rarely will a non-believer ever pick up a Bible to read and learn about God. Rarely will they read a Christian book or watch Christian television. Believers are the only message non-believers will likely receive from the Lord. What is the message of our lives to those who do not believe?

The Greater Glory of the New Covenant

3:5-15: This must qualify as one of the remarkable texts in the New Testament. We are told here that the glory of the New Covenant is greater than that of the Old Covenant, and therefore, we should be experiencing even more glory than Moses did. One of the ultimate questions we should be asking is, "Where is the glory?" Certainly God spoke to Moses face to face, but we have something better than that—we have God living inside of us! Do our lives reflect this greatest of all wonders? Do our lives have the glory of God on them?

The Glory that Changes Us

3:16-18: If we are indeed beholding the glory of the Lord, then we will be transformed into His same image. If we are beholding Him and following Him, then His glory will be seen in us.

NOTES:

PAUL'S SECOND LETTER TO THE
CORINTHIANS
II Corinthians 4

Apostolic Endurance

1 Therefore seeing that we have this ministry, even as we obtained mercy, we do not grow weary,

2 but we have renounced the hidden things of shame, not walking in craftiness, nor handling the Word of God deceitfully, but by the manifestation of the truth we commend ourselves to every man's conscience in the sight of God.

3 If our gospel is veiled it is veiled to those who are perishing,

4 whom the god of this world has blinded so that with their minds they are not able to believe. This is so that the light of the gospel of the glory of Christ, who is the image of God, will not dawn upon them.

5 We do not preach ourselves, but Christ Jesus as Lord, and ourselves as your servants for Jesus' sake.

6 Seeing it is God that said, "Light will shine out of the darkness," who shined this light in our hearts to give the light of the knowledge of the glory of God in the face of Jesus Christ.

7 However, we have this treasure in earthen vessels, so that the exceeding greatness of the power may be from God, and not from ourselves.

8 We are pressed on every side, yet not overcome. We are perplexed at times, and yet do not despair.

9 We are persecuted, yet we know we are not forsaken. We have been beaten down, but not destroyed.

10 We always bear in our body the dying of Jesus, so that the life of Jesus may also be manifested in our body.

11 For we who live are constantly being delivered over to death for Jesus' sake, so that the life of Jesus also may be manifested in our mortal flesh.

12 So then death works in us, but life in you.

Living for the Resurrection

13 Now, having the same spirit of faith, according to that which is written, I believed, and therefore I speak out.

14 We know that He who raised the Lord Jesus will raise us also with Jesus, and will present us together with you.

15 For all things are for your sake, that the grace, being multiplied through the many, may cause the thanksgiving to abound to the glory of God.

16 Therefore we do not grow weary, but though our outward man is decaying, yet our inner man is being renewed day by day.

17 For our light affliction that is for but a moment works for us increasingly, and exceedingly, an eternal weight of glory.

18 For we do not look at the things which are seen, but at the things which are not seen, because the things that are seen are temporal, but the things that are not seen are eternal.

Apostolic Endurance

II Corinthians 4:1-12: This is one of the great insights into how the most basic element of the Christian faith—that Christ gave His own life so that we might live—is practically walked out by the messengers of this gospel, by laying down their lives for others. His messengers live a life of sacrifice so that others might find life. The degree to which we lay down our lives for Him is the degree to which His life flows through us.

Living for the Resurrection

4:13-18: What enables the messengers of the gospel to live sacrificially is their faith in the resurrection. The degree to which

we really believe the gospel will be reflected in our willingness to sacrifice for the Lord and His people.

NOTES:

Paul's Second Letter To The
CORINTHIANS
II Corinthians 5

At Home in the Spirit

1   For we know that if our earthly house, our tabernacle, deteriorates, we have a building from God, a house not made with hands, eternal, in the heavens.

2   For truly in this body we groan, longing to be clothed with our habitation that is from heaven,

3   and being clothed we will not be found naked.

4   For indeed we who are in this tabernacle do groan, being burdened, not to be unclothed, but that we would be clothed, so that which is mortal may be swallowed up in life.

5   Now He who created us for this very thing is God, who gave to us the deposit of the Spirit.

6   Therefore, always being of good courage, and knowing that, while we are at home in the body, we are absent from the Lord,

7   because we walk by faith, not by sight.

8   We are of good courage, and are willing rather to be absent from the body to be at home with the Lord.

9   Therefore, it is our desire, whether at home or absent, to be well-pleasing to Him.

All Things for His Sake

10   For we must all stand before the judgment seat of Christ so that each one may receive what is deserved for the things done in the body, according to whether he has done good or evil.

11   Therefore, knowing the fear of the Lord we seek to persuade men, but we live our lives before God, and I hope that we are also made manifest in your consciences.

12 We are not again commending ourselves to you, but as giving you occasion for glorying on our behalf, that you may have an answer for those who glory in appearances, and not in heart.

13 If we are out of our minds it is for God, or if we are of a sober mind, it is for you.

14 The love of Christ controls us because we are mindful of this one thing; that one died for all, therefore all were under the sentence of death.

15 He died for all so that they that live should no longer live for themselves, but for Him who died for their sakes, and rose again.

16 Therefore, from now on we know no man after the flesh, even though we have known Christ after the flesh, yet we do not know Him this way any longer.

17 If any man is in Christ, he is a new creature, the old things have passed away, and all things have become new.

The Ministry of Reconciliation

18 All things are from God, who reconciled us to Himself through Christ, and gave to us the ministry of reconciliation.

19 God was in Christ reconciling the world to Himself, not reckoning their trespasses against them, and having committed to us the word of reconciliation.

20 Therefore, we are ambassadors for Christ, as though God were entreating through us we beseech you on behalf of Christ, be reconciled to God.

21 Him who knew no sin He made to be sin on our behalf so that we might become the righteousness of God in Him.

At Home in the Spirit

II Corinthians 5:1-9: The new-creation man is both natural and spiritual. As we are being transformed into spiritual rather than natural beings, we begin to long for our spiritual bodies. As this process continues, there is a point we start feeling more at home in the spiritual realm than the natural realm. This is evidence of spiritual maturity for all who are born again by the

Spirit. It is evidence of spiritual maturity when we walk more by what we see with "the eyes of our heart," our spiritual eyes, than we do with our natural eyes. That is walking by faith.

All Things for His Sake

5:10-17: For depth and content, these few verses may be the most extraordinary in Scripture. In them, we are told that:

We must all stand before the judgment seat of Christ

The love of Christ controls us

He died for all so that those who live should no longer live for themselves

From now on, we know no man after the flesh

If any man is in Christ, he is a new creature

Certainly, we could spend many days just pondering these few verses. How would we live if we truly walked in the knowledge that we will all stand before the judgment seat of Christ? Does the love of Christ really control us, or are we motivated mostly by lesser purposes and the temporary things of this life? Do we really live for Him or for ourselves? Do we recognize people by their character rather than race, culture, denomination, or other external matters? Are we truly living as a new creation? To walk in the truth of these verses is the highest goal we can have in this life and sums up the greatest success we can have in this life.

The Ministry of Reconciliation

5:18-21: The result of walking the true spiritual life is that we become ambassadors of Christ. We represent Him in His ultimate purpose of reconciling the world back to God. In biblical times, being an ambassador was the highest honor a king or emperor could give someone. This was because communication between the potentate and his ambassadors could take months of travel in each direction. Therefore, only one's very best friends would be sent as ambassadors, those who shared complete unity of heart and mind and would represent him appropriately. Can our King trust us to represent Him in this same way?

NOTES:

Paul's Second Letter To The
CORINTHIANS
II Corinthians 6

Apostolic Trials

1 Working together with Him we entreat you not to receive the grace of God in vain

2 for He says, **"At an acceptable time I listened to you, and in a day of salvation I helped you. Behold, now is the acceptable time; behold, now is the day of salvation" (Isaiah 49:8).**

3 We gave no occasion for an offense in anything so that our ministry is not blamed for being a stumbling block to those who do not receive His grace.

4 In everything we are commending ourselves as ministers of God, in much patience, in afflictions, in need, in distresses,

5 in stripes, in imprisonments, in riots, in labors, in watching, in fasting;

6 in pureness, in knowledge, in patience, in kindness, in the Holy Spirit, in unfeigned love,

7 in the word of truth, in the power of God, by the armor of righteousness on the right hand and on the left,

8 whether in glory or dishonor, by evil report or good report. We are called deceivers, and yet we are true.

9 We are as unknown, and yet well known, as dying, but behold, we live. We are chastened, but not killed,

10 sorrowful, yet always rejoicing. We are poor, yet are making many rich, having nothing, and yet possessing all things.

11 Our mouth is open to you, O Corinthians, as our heart is enlarged.

12 You are not restrained by us, but you are restrained by your own affections.

13 Now for a repayment in like kind (I speak as to my children), so that you will also enlarged.

Be Equally Yoked

14 Do not be unequally yoked with unbelievers, because what fellowship has righteousness with iniquity? Or what communion has light with darkness?

15 What agreement has Christ with Belial? Or what portion has a believer with an unbeliever?

16 What agreement has a temple of God with idols? For we are a temple of the living God, even as God said, **"I will dwell with them, and walk with them; and I will be their God, and they shall be my people"** (see Exodus 25:8, 29:45; Leviticus 26:12; Jeremiah 31:1; Ezekiel 37:27).

17 **"Therefore, 'Come out from among them, and be separate,' says the Lord, 'Do not touch any unclean thing, and I will receive you,**

18 **"'and will be a Father to you, and you shall be sons and daughters to Me', says the Lord Almighty"** (see Isaiah 43:6; Hosea 1:10).

Apostolic Trials

II Corinthians 6:1-13: First-century apostles lived hard lives. They were continually persecuted and under threat of attack. Being an apostle required one to die daily to any personal ambitions or desires. The drive of their lives had to be love for God, love for people, and an unrelenting devotion to make Him and His gospel known. We are in need of such great and noble souls of this stature today.

Be Equally Yoked

6:14-18: If the love of Christ controls us and He is our first love, then to be yoked with unbelievers would not even be a consideration. Our first love requires that we do all things for the sake of His gospel. This is not just when considering marriage, but other partnerships as well.

NOTES:

PAUL'S SECOND LETTER TO THE
CORINTHIANS
II Corinthians 7

Comfort One Another

1   Therefore, having these promises, beloved, let us cleanse ourselves from all defilement of flesh and spirit, seeking to perfect holiness in the fear of God.

2   Open your hearts to us. We have not wronged anyone, corrupted anyone, or taken advantage of anyone.

3   I do not say this to condemn you, for as I have said before, you are in our hearts whether to die together or to live together.

4   Great is my boldness of speech toward you, but also great is my glorying on your behalf. I am filled with comfort. I overflow with joy in all of our affliction.

5   For even when we had come into Macedonia our flesh had no relief, but we were afflicted on every side. We had conflicts without, fears within.

6   Nevertheless He that comforts the lowly, even God, comforted us by the coming of Titus.

7   Not just by his coming, but also by the comfort wherewith he was comforted by you, when he told us of your longing, your mourning, your zeal for me, so that I rejoiced even more.

Godly Sorrow

8   For though I made you sorrowful with my letter, I do not regret it, though I did regret it, but now I see that the letter made you sorrowful for only a season.

9   I now rejoice, not that you were made sorrowful, but that you were made sorrowful to the point of repentance. For you were made

sorrowful with a godly sorrow so that you might not suffer loss in anything.

10 For godly sorrow brings repentance that leads to salvation, which does not result in regret, but the sorrow of the world brings death.

11 For this godly sorrow produced in you a great zeal, a determination to clear yourselves, an indignation, a fear, and a longing and desire to be avenged! In everything you proved to be righteous in the matter.

12 So although I wrote to you, I did not write for the cause of the one who did wrong, nor for his cause that suffered the wrong, but that your earnest care for us might be made manifest in the sight of God.

13 Therefore we have been comforted, and in our comfort we had joy even more exceedingly because of the joy of Titus, because his spirit was refreshed by you.

14 For if in anything I have boasted to him on your behalf, I was not put to shame, but as we spoke all things to you in truth, so our glorying also that I made before Titus was found to be truth.

15 Now his affection is even greater toward you, while he remembers the obedience of you all, how with fear and trembling you received him.

16 I rejoice that in everything I have courage concerning you.

Comfort One Another

II Corinthians 7:1-7: Paul was a tough, resolute, and uncompromising apostle, but this only made his tenderness and affection for his spiritual children even more powerful. Their love for him became a great source of his joy.

Godly Sorrow

7:8-16: There is a godly sorrow and a worldly sorrow. Godly sorrow results in repentance, which is turning to God. Ungodly sorrow is a discouragement that turns our focus inward so we feel sorry for ourselves and become discouraged. Self-pity is the ultimate form of selfishness. It is a spiritual black hole that few who fall deeply into ever get back out of. The object is not to avoid sorrow, but to deeply feel the right kind of sorrow, when

necessary. **The result should turn us to God, not inward and into the trap of self-pity.**

NOTES:

Paul's Second Letter To The
CORINTHIANS
II Corinthians 8

Faith of the Macedonians

1 Moreover, brethren, we make known to you the grace of God that has been given to the churches of Macedonia.

2 This is demonstrated by how they endured much testing, and through their afflictions the abundance of their joy caused their deep poverty to abound with riches because of their liberality.

3 I bear witness that according to their means, and beyond their means, they gave of their own accord,

4 asking us with much entreaty to participate in the fellowship in ministering to the saints.

5 They gave beyond what we had hoped, but first they gave their own selves to the Lord, and to us through the will of God.

6 This compelled us to exhort Titus, that as he made a beginning before, so he would also complete in you this grace also.

The Grace of Generosity

7 As you abound in everything, in faith, and utterance, and knowledge, and in all earnestness, and in your love for us, see that you abound in this grace also.

8 I do not speak by way of commandment, but as proving through the earnestness of others the sincerity also of your love.

9 For you know the grace of our Lord Jesus Christ, that, even though He was rich, yet for your sakes he became poor, that you, through His poverty, might become rich.

10 In this I give my judgment, which is expedient for you, who were the first to begin this a year ago, not only to do it, but also to have a heart for it.

11 Now complete the doing also, that as there was the readiness of heart, so there may be the completion also out of your ability.

12 For if the readiness is there, it is acceptable according as a man has, not according do what he does not have.

13 For this is not just so that others may be at ease and you be distressed,

14 but by equality in that your abundance is being made a supply at this present time for their needs, that their abundance also may become a supply for your needs, so that there may be equality.

15 As it is written, **"He that gathered much had nothing left over; and he that gathered little had no lack" (see Exodus 16:18).**

16 Thanks be to God who puts the same earnest care for you into the heart of Titus.

17 For he accepted our exhortation, but being himself very earnest, he went to you of his own accord.

18 We have sent together with him the brother whose praise in the gospel has spread through all the churches.

Faith with Honor

19 Not only so, but who was also appointed by the churches to travel with us in the matter of this grace, which is ministered by us to the glory of the Lord, and to show our readiness.

20 We seek to avoid giving an opportunity for any man to blame us in the matter of this bounty that is ministered by us.

21 For this reason we take thought for the things that are honorable, not only in the sight of the Lord, but also in the sight of men.

22 We have sent with them our brother, whom we have many times proved trustworthy, but now is much more earnest by reason of the great confidence which he has in you.

23 If any have questions about Titus, he is my partner and my fellow-worker for your sake. As brethren, they are the messengers of the churches; they are the glory of Christ.

24 Therefore show the proof of your love to them before the churches, and justify our glorying on your behalf.

Faith of the Macedonians

II Corinthians 8:1-6: When we experience the unfathomable gift of God, then we too will become generous, as His nature is manifested in us. The more we mature in Christ, the more we become like Him, and the more gracious and generous we will be.

The Grace of Generosity

8:7-18: The remarkable generosity of the Corinthian church, even in the midst of persecution and impoverishment, became a testimony and made their church famous throughout the world at the time. What is your church known for?

Faith with Honor

8:19-24: Here we see messengers who were "sent by the churches." The churches had the authority in Christ to send apostles. These were of a different category than those sent directly by the Lord, such as the twelve and Paul. Even so, they were recognized by the Lord and His people. In modern times, the title of apostle has become very common and many who claim it may well be like those who were sent by the churches. However, there is a great difference in the authority of one sent by the churches, and one who has been ordained and sent directly by the Lord.

We must also recognize that there are many "false apostles," those who have sent themselves and claimed this position for themselves. The Lord commended those in the church of Ephesus who had put these so-called apostles to the test and found them to be false (see Revelation 2:2). We must do the same, or the damage the church incurs will be great.

NOTES:

PAUL'S SECOND LETTER TO THE
CORINTHIANS
II Corinthians 9

The Reward of Generosity

1   It is superfluous for me to write to you about the ministry to the saints

2   because I know your readiness. I glory on your behalf about this to those who are in Macedonia, that Achaia has been prepared for the past year, and your zeal inspired many of them.

3   So I have sent the brethren ahead for this reason, to insure that our glorying on your behalf may not be in vain, and just as I said, you may be prepared.

4   This is in case some come with me from Macedonia and find you unprepared, in which we, as well as you, should be put to shame by our boasting.

5   I thought it necessary therefore to entreat the brethren so that they would go before us to prepare beforehand your promised bountiful gift, so that it might be ready. This is because of your generosity, not because of any pressure to do so.

6   It is written, that he who sows sparingly will also reap sparingly, and he that sows bountifully will also reap bountifully.

7   Therefore, let each man do just as he has purposed in his heart, not grudgingly, or under compulsion, because God loves a cheerful giver.

8   Then God is able to make all grace abound to you so that you always have all sufficiency in everything, and you may have an abundance for every good work.

9   It is written, **"He has scattered abroad, he has given to the poor; His righteousness abides forever" (see Psalm 112:9).**

10 So He who supplies seed to the sower, and bread for food, will supply and multiply your seed for sowing, and increase the harvest of your righteousness.

11 This is so that you will be enriched in everything for your generosity, which works through us that many will be thankful to God.

12 For the administration of this ministry not only meets the needs of the saints, but abounds also through many to produce thanksgiving to God,

13 seeing that through the proving of you by this administration they glorify God for the obedience to your confession to the gospel of Christ, and for the liberality of your contribution to them, and to all.

14 They themselves also, with prayers on your behalf, long after you by reason of the exceeding grace of God in you.

15 Thanks be to God for His indescribable gift.

The Reward of Generosity

II Corinthians 9:1-15: This is one of the central chapters in The Bible about the basic grace of generosity. As the apostle explains, this is the path to a truly prosperous life. Those who faithfully practice generosity will be a demonstration of the power and character of the New Covenant, always abounding and overflowing for good deeds. Generosity and charity are rare, except in Christianized nations. In those nations, the greatest charity inevitably comes from those who are the most zealous for the Lord because the foundation of Christianity is that God so loved the world that He gave His best to us, His Son. Those who are growing up into Him become like Him. Giving their best, they demonstrate the highest purpose of man, which is to love God and one another. Love loves to give!

NOTES:

Paul's Second Letter To The
CORINTHIANS
II Corinthians 10

Using Spiritual Weapons

1 Now I Paul entreat you by the meekness and gentleness of Christ, I who in your presence am humble and meek, but being absent am bold toward you.

2 Yes, I beseech you, that I may not have to show boldness in your presence with the confidence whereby I could be bold toward some, who consider us as if we walked according to the flesh.

3 For though we walk in the flesh, we do not war according to the flesh.

4 The weapons of our warfare are not carnal, but are divinely powerful for the casting down of strongholds.

5 They cast down imaginations, and every high thing that exalts itself against the knowledge of God, and will bring every thought into captivity, into obedience to Christ.

6 We will be ready to avenge all disobedience when your obedience is complete.

7 Look at the things that are before your face. If any man trusts in himself that he is Christ's, let him consider this again within himself, even as he is Christ's, so also are we.

Authority to Build Up or Tear Down

8 For though I boast somewhat abundantly concerning our authority that the Lord gave me for building you up, and not for tearing you down, I will not be put to shame.

9 It may seem that I would terrify you by my letters,

10 as they say "his letters are weighty and strong, but his physical presence is weak, and his speech is not impressive."

11 Let such a one consider this, that, what we are in word by letters when absent, we are the same in deed when we are present.

12 For we are not bold because we are like certain ones who commend themselves, but when they use themselves as a standard of measure, and compare themselves with each other, they are without understanding.

Spheres of Authority

13 We will not boast beyond our measure, but according to the measure of the sphere of authority that God apportioned to us as a measure, to reach even as far as you.

14 For we do not go beyond the sphere of authority that has been assigned to us, as though we did not reach to you, for we took the gospel of Christ even as far as to you.

15 So we are not boasting beyond our measure, which we would be if we were boasting in other men's labors, but having hope that, as your faith grows, we will be magnified by you so that our sphere of authority is increased.

16 Then we would be able to preach the gospel even to the regions beyond you, and not to boast in another's accomplishments that were not done by our own hand.

17 But he that glories, let him glory in the Lord.

18 For it is not he who commends himself that is approved, but whom the Lord commends.

Using Spiritual Weapons

II Corinthians 10:1-7: Our spiritual weapons are more powerful than any guns, bombs, or missiles. Nothing has ever changed men or nations like the truth spoken in love under the anointing. This not only changes people's minds, but their mindsets—the very way that they think. As difficulties in the last days continue to unfold, those who walk in the peace and joy of the Lord, the fruit of life lived in truth, will stand out as even brighter lights.

Authority to Build Up or Tear Down

10:8-12: Paul had the authority to build up or to tear down because he was the one God used to build them up in Christ. Some presume the authority to tear down where they have not done the building. These are the stumbling blocks we have been warned about.

Spheres of Authority

10:13-18: There are spheres of authority that are dictated by the Lord, and their boundaries are indicated by where we have fruit. When we presume to go beyond the boundaries we are given, there will be unnecessary trouble. We see this when Peter, who was called to the Jews, went to the Gentiles in Antioch and fell into hypocrisy. Likewise, when Paul, who was called to the Gentiles, tried to go to the Jews, it did not work out very well, though God still used it. God will bless all that we do as much as He can, but the greatest fruit will always come from being in His will and staying in the place where He has given us authority.

NOTES:

PAUL'S SECOND LETTER TO THE
CORINTHIANS
II Corinthians 11

Jealousy for the Bride

1 I would that you could bear with me in a little foolishness, but indeed you do bear with me.

2 For I am jealous over you with a godly jealousy, because I espoused you to one husband, that I might present you as a pure virgin to Christ.

3 But I fear that just as the serpent beguiled Eve by his craftiness that by various means your minds should be corrupted and led astray from the simplicity of pure devotion to Christ.

4 For if he that comes preaches another Jesus whom we did not preach, or if you receive a different spirit that you did not receive, or a different gospel, that you did not accept, you do bear it well.

5 For I am not in any way inferior to the most imminent apostles.

6 Though I am not eloquent in speech, am I less in knowledge? No. In every way we have made this manifest to you in all things.

7 Or did I commit a sin in abasing myself that you might be exalted, because I preached the gospel of God to you without charge?

8 I robbed other churches, taking wages from them that I might minister to you.

9 When I was present with you and was in need, I was not a burden on any man, because when the brethren came from Macedonia, they supplied all of my needs. In everything I kept myself from being burdensome to you, and so I will continue.

10 As the truth of Christ is in me no man can refute this testimony that I have in the regions of Achaia.

11 Is this because I do not love you? God knows that I do.

False Workers

12 What I do I will do so that I may prevent an opportunity to those who seek an occasion to undermine our work in you, which they do to find an occasion to seem equal to us.

13 For such men are false apostles, deceitful workers, fashioning themselves into apostles of Christ.

14 Do not marvel at this because even Satan makes himself into an angel of light.

15 It is not unexpected then that his ministers would also fashion themselves as ministers of righteousness, whose end will be according to their works.

16 I say again, let no man think of me as foolish, but if you do, then receive me as one who is foolish, that I also may glory a little.

17 That which I speak, I do not speak as from the Lord, but as in jesting, but I do have confidence in my boasting.

18 Seeing that many boast about matters of the flesh, so in this I will boast also.

19 For you bear with the foolish gladly, being wise yourselves.

20 For you endure a man if he brings you into bondage, if he devours you, if he takes advantage of you, if he exalts himself, if he hits you in the face.

21 I speak by way of disparagement, as though we had been weak. Yet in whatever anyone is bold, (I am still jesting), I am bold also.

Evidence of Paul's Apostleship

22 Are they Hebrews? So am I. Are they Israelites? So am I. Are they the seed of Abraham? So am I.

23 Are they ministers of Christ? (I speak as one beside himself), I am even more so; in more abundant labors, having been imprisoned more often, in stripes above measure, in the deep often.

24 From the Jews I received thirty-nine lashes five times,

25 and three times I was beaten with rods, once was I stoned, three times I suffered shipwreck, I have spent a night and a day in the deep.

26 I am on frequent journeys, in danger on rivers, in danger from robbers, in danger from my countrymen, in danger from the Gentiles, in danger in the city, in danger from the wilderness, in danger on the sea, in danger from false brethren.

27 I am constantly in labor and travail, in watchings, hungry and thirsty, often fasting, in both cold and nakedness.

28 Besides those things that are without, there is one matter that burdens me daily: concern for all the churches.

29 Who is weak, and I am not weak? Who is caused to stumble, and I do not grieve?

30 If I need to boast or glory, I will boast of the things that concern my weakness.

31 The God and Father of the Lord Jesus, He who is blessed for evermore, knows that I do not lie.

32 In Damascus the governor under Aretas the king guarded the city in order to seize me,

33 and I was let down in a basket through a window in the wall, and escaped his hands.

Jealousy for the Bride

II Corinthians 11:1-11: There is a difference between being possessive of the work of God out of personal selfishness and being jealous for the Lord's sake. When we are driven to be possessive out of selfishness, we are in danger of becoming what Paul warned of—false workers. True workers are servants of Jesus Christ and are not motivated by personal gain. They do not consider the work of the Lord their possession, but His.

We see that some can preach the deception of "another Jesus," or "another gospel." An obvious example of this is the Jesus portrayed in the Koran, who is a different Jesus from the Jesus of the New Testament. Neither is the Allah of the Koran the Jehovah of The Bible, though many claim them to be the same. We must not be fooled by people who use His name, yet are not preaching the truth of Christ but rather "another gospel."

As Paul warned in verse 3, a basic deception comes when we depart from the simplicity of devotion to Christ. This is the same deception by which the serpent deceived Eve in the Garden. In all our work for Christ, we must keep it simple—love Him, and do His will for the sake of His gospel.

False Workers

11:12-21: There are false workers who come disguised as messengers of truth and righteousness. This was true throughout the church age, just as the Lord warned in His parable of the wheat and tares. One way the false ones are almost always exposed is their overbearing leadership, arrogance in exalting themselves, and taking advantage of people (see verse 20). When this nature surfaces in anyone, they must be rejected as apostles or leaders in the church. True shepherds will take authority to protect the flock of God from such as these.

We must also consider that one can be a false apostle, but be a true brother. Many true Christians have presumed positions and titles beyond what they have received from the Lord, yet they may be true believers in Christ. Even so, as Jesus commended the Ephesian church in the Book of Revelation for putting to the test those who called themselves apostles and were not, we must do the same. One of the tragedies of recent times has been that many leaders now claim to be apostles, yet they are not apostolic in depth, authority, or character. We will be blessed if we have the integrity to protect the work of God, as well as protect the spiritual currency of the true apostolic ministry by being willing to challenge those who walk in presumption.

Evidence of Paul's Apostleship

11:22-33: In defending his apostleship, Paul did not point to things he had accomplished, but rather to the afflictions he suffered for the sake of the gospel. This is because the real evidence of true laborers is the cross they take up continually for the One who took up His cross for them.

NOTES:

Paul's Second Letter To The
CORINTHIANS
II Corinthians 12

Paul's Revelations

1   If I must boast, though it is not expedient, I will speak of visions and revelations of the Lord.

2   I know a man in Christ who, fourteen years ago, whether in the body, or whether out of the body, I do not know; God knows, but such a one was caught up to the third heaven.

3   I know such a man whether in the body, or apart from the body, I do not know, but God knows,

4   how he was caught up into Paradise, and heard words that cannot be expressed, which it is not lawful for a man to declare.

5   On behalf of such a one I will boast, but on my own behalf I will not boast, except in my weaknesses.

6   For if I desire to boast I would not do it in jesting. I will speak the truth, but be patient with me, so that no man will take me to be more than what he sees in me, or hears from me.

A Thorn in the Flesh

7   It was because of the exceeding greatness of the revelations that I have received a thorn in the flesh that was given to me so that I would not be overly exalted. *This was* a messenger from Satan to buffet me so that I would not become arrogant.

8   Concerning this thing I inquired of the Lord three times that it might depart from me.

9   He said to me, "My grace is sufficient for you, because My power is made perfect in weakness." Most gladly, therefore, I would rather boast in my weaknesses, that the power of Christ may rest upon me.

10 Therefore, I take pleasure in weaknesses, in injuries, in needs, in persecutions, in distresses, for Christ's sake, because when I am weak, then I am strong because of His power that works in me.

11 I have become foolish, but it was because you compelled me. For I should have been commended by you, for in nothing was I less than the very chief apostles, though I am nothing.

The Power of an Apostle's Love

12 Truly the signs of an apostle were wrought among you in all patience, by signs and wonders and mighty works.

13 For in what were you made inferior to the rest of the churches, except that I myself was not a burden to you? Forgive me for this wrong!

14 Behold, this is the third time I am ready to come to you, and I will not be a burden to you this time either. I do not seek what is yours, but you. For the children should not have to provide for their parents, but the parents provide for their children.

15 I will most gladly spend and be spent for your souls. If I love you more abundantly, am I loved the less?

16 But let it be so, I did not burden you myself, but, being the crafty fellow that I am, I caught you with guile.

17 Did I take advantage of you by any one of the ones whom I have sent to you?

18 I exhorted Titus, and I sent the brother with him. Did Titus take advantage of you? Did we not come in the same spirit? Did we not behave in the same way?

19 You think all this time that we are excusing ourselves to you. In the sight of God we speak in Christ. All of these things, beloved, are for your edifying.

20 For I fear, that in any way, when I come, I should not find you such as I would, and should myself be found by you not as you expect, lest by any means there should be strife, jealousy, wrath, factions, betrayals, gossip, arrogance, conflicts;

21 lest again when I come my God should humble me before you, and I should mourn for many of those who have sinned, and did not

repent of the uncleanness, and fornication, and lasciviousness which they committed.

Paul's Revelations

II Corinthians 12:1-6: Most theologians think that the "man" Paul refers to, who had these great revelations and was caught up into the third heaven, was himself. This discourse leads to many other questions, such as: If there is a third heaven, is there a first and second, or maybe even a fourth, fifth, etc.?

Of course, there could be realms of heaven described this way, but some teachers and theologians have an interesting concept of this. They believe that "the third heaven" is describing the time of the millennium in which Christ will reign over the earth. They say this because we are told that the first heavens and earth were destroyed during the flood, which would make the age we are presently living in the time of the second heavens and earth. The next age would be the third. To clarify, the "heaven" and "earth" are not referring to the literal terra firma, or air, or even heavenly realms themselves, but rather to the authorities over them during these periods. In this age, we know that Satan is the "prince of the air," or the one who reigns in the heavenly realm over the earth, but he will be displaced by Christ in the next age.

Others see this "third heaven" as being a literal realm of heaven that is higher than the first two. These consider the "first heaven" the physical heavens about which The Bible has much to say. The "second heavens" are considered the spiritual realm over the earth. This realm is dominated by Satan with his principalities and powers during this age, but will be replaced by Christ in the age to come. The "third heaven" is the highest spiritual realm revealed in Scripture. It is the realm over which God now abides. There is merit to this view as well, just as there is to most of the theories pertaining to what Paul described here.

Some great teachers and theologians in history held very lightly to their beliefs about what Paul said in these verses. What we believe about these things is certainly not essential doctrine.

Therefore, it is best to leave it just that way, for it has only been revealed in part. We take from it what we can, but we do not speculate about what is not clearly revealed.

From the time I was a new believer, I was personally interested in these experiences and prayed to have them. I prayed to be caught up to see the third heaven as Paul described. I did not see anywhere in Scripture where we could not do this, and I had a great desire for it. So I figured, why not? It began to happen after twenty-five years of praying. In some of these experiences, I felt as if I had literally been carried into a new realm. Yet I also knew that prophetic experiences could seem like you were really transported somewhere else, not that you left your body or this physical realm. Then I fully understood what Paul mentioned about not knowing if he was in the body or not. Even so, I saw many things that I thought were beyond any earthly imagination.

In that realm, I also heard and understood communication between all living things. It seemed that all things were alive. In that place, I came to understand that love was the food that all life was fueled by. I don't think it was possible to even look at something or someone without loving them and having abounding joy in them. There was also a communication with all things that transcended words. This may have been what Paul was talking about when he said he heard words that could not be expressed. This communication was on a higher level than words. As well as knowing the thoughts being conveyed, I felt every emotion and could understand their communication exactly. It was a communication that could not be expressed in present human language because it was so spiritual.

Regardless of our experiences and revelations, these are not a cause for boasting. They are not evidence of our maturity, authority, or holiness. They too come by grace. We do not become holy in order to see the Lord, but we are made holy by seeing Him.

Because this is a mistake frequently made by believers, I often repeat that prophetic experiences are never to be the basis of any church doctrine. Only the written Word of God is used for that. Such revelations can be helpful in understanding the times and preparing us for them, but if we boast, let us boast in the Lord. All pride will lead to a fall.

A Thorn in the Flesh

11:7-11: Paul's thorn in the flesh is a mystery. A "messenger of Satan" would be a demon. Therefore, most consider that this was a particular demonic attack Paul suffered to buffet him and keep him humble. Some believe it was a person who was demonized, or demonically influenced, and that this person followed Paul everywhere. Notwithstanding, Paul was of such high spiritual authority with many great revelations that he might have needed some help to stay humble. Humility is required for receiving the grace of God. The grace of great revelation or authority can be accompanied by a "thorn in the flesh," which is the grace of God to help us remain humble.

We are told throughout Scripture to humble ourselves. If we would have a resolve to obey this, never promoting or exalting ourselves, then we might not need humbling by outside forces or circumstances. Humility is always right. It is better to think less of oneself rather than more, and to let the Lord do any exalting as He sees fit to do.

The Power of an Apostle's Love

11:12-21: Paul concluded his exhortation by mourning over their carnality—strife, jealousy, wrath, factions, gossip, pride, uncleanness, fornication, and so on. He knew that his great revelations meant little if he could not compel God's people to live rightly before Him, walking in the Spirit and not the flesh. These will be the jewels in our crown on that great judgment day, not our revelations.

NOTES:

Paul's Second Letter To The
CORINTHIANS
II Corinthians 13

The Test of Faith

1   This is the third time I am coming to you. From the mouth of two or three witnesses let every word be established.

2   I have said before, and I say again just as when I was present the second time, so now being absent, to those who have sinned before, and to all the rest, that if I come again I will not spare anyone.

3   Seeing that you seek a proof of Christ that speaks in me, who is not weak toward you, but is powerful.

4   He was crucified because of weakness, yet He lives through the power of God. For we are also weak in Him but we will live with Him through the power of God.

5   Test yourselves to see whether you are in the faith. Prove yourselves. Or do you not know that Jesus Christ is in you? That is unless you are a reprobate and fail the test.

6   I hope that you know that we do not fail the test.

7   Now we pray to God that you do no evil, not just so that we may appear approved, but that you may do that which is honorable even if we were to become reprobates.

8   For we can do nothing against the truth, but only for the truth.

9   For we rejoice when we are weak, and you are strong. We pray for your perfecting.

10 For this cause I write these things while absent, that I may not have to deal harshly when present, according to the authority the Lord gave me for building up, and not for tearing down.

11 Finally, brethren, farewell. Be perfected, be comforted, be of the same mind, live in peace, and the God of love and peace will be with you.

12 Salute one another with a holy kiss.

13 All the saints salute you.

14 The grace of the Lord Jesus Christ, and the love of God, and the communion of the Holy Spirit, be with you all.

The Test of Faith

II Corinthians 13:1-14: In this conclusion, Paul reminded them of his authority to bring correction, if necessary. However, he would prefer that they did this for themselves—test themselves to see if they were in the faith. There is a place for evaluating our spiritual state and our progress toward maturity. We measure ourselves by the Lord, who we are called to grow up into in all things. Are we becoming more Christlike? Are we growing in faith, love, and patience? This is far more important than advancing in any profession, because how we grow spiritually will last forever.

In verse 7, Paul made a statement that should be the hallmark of all true ministry. He said that even if he was to become reprobate, the Corinthians would press on in Christ. If we are truly building upon the only foundation that will stand, Christ Himself, then even if we who build should fall away, that which we have built should remain. Why is it that when leaders fall, most of those whom they led fall too? It is because those leaders built on their own ministry, gifts, charisma, knowledge, etc., rather than on Christ. True apostles build on Christ, not themselves. The warning to build only on Christ is a fitting conclusion to this great letter.

NOTES:

Paul's Second Letter to the Corinthians Proper Names and Meanings

Abraham: father of a multitude, exalted father

Achaia: grief, trouble

Aretas: agreeable, virtuous

Asia: muddy, boggy

Belial: wicked, worthless

Christ: anointed

Corinth: satisfied, ornament, beauty

Damascus: a sack full of blood, the similitude of burning, silent is the sackcloth weaver

Eve: living, enlivening, life giver

Gentiles: the nations or pagan

Hebrews: descendants of Heber

Israel: who prevails with God, prince of God

Israelites: descendants of Israel, prevails with God

Jesus: savior, deliverer, Yahweh is salvation

Macedonia: burning, adoration

Moses: taken out, drawn forth

Paradise: park, orchard

Paul: small

Satan: contrary, adversary, enemy, accuser, deceiver

Silvanus: who loves the forest

Titus: pleasing

Troas: penetrated

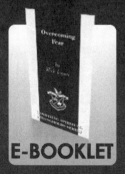

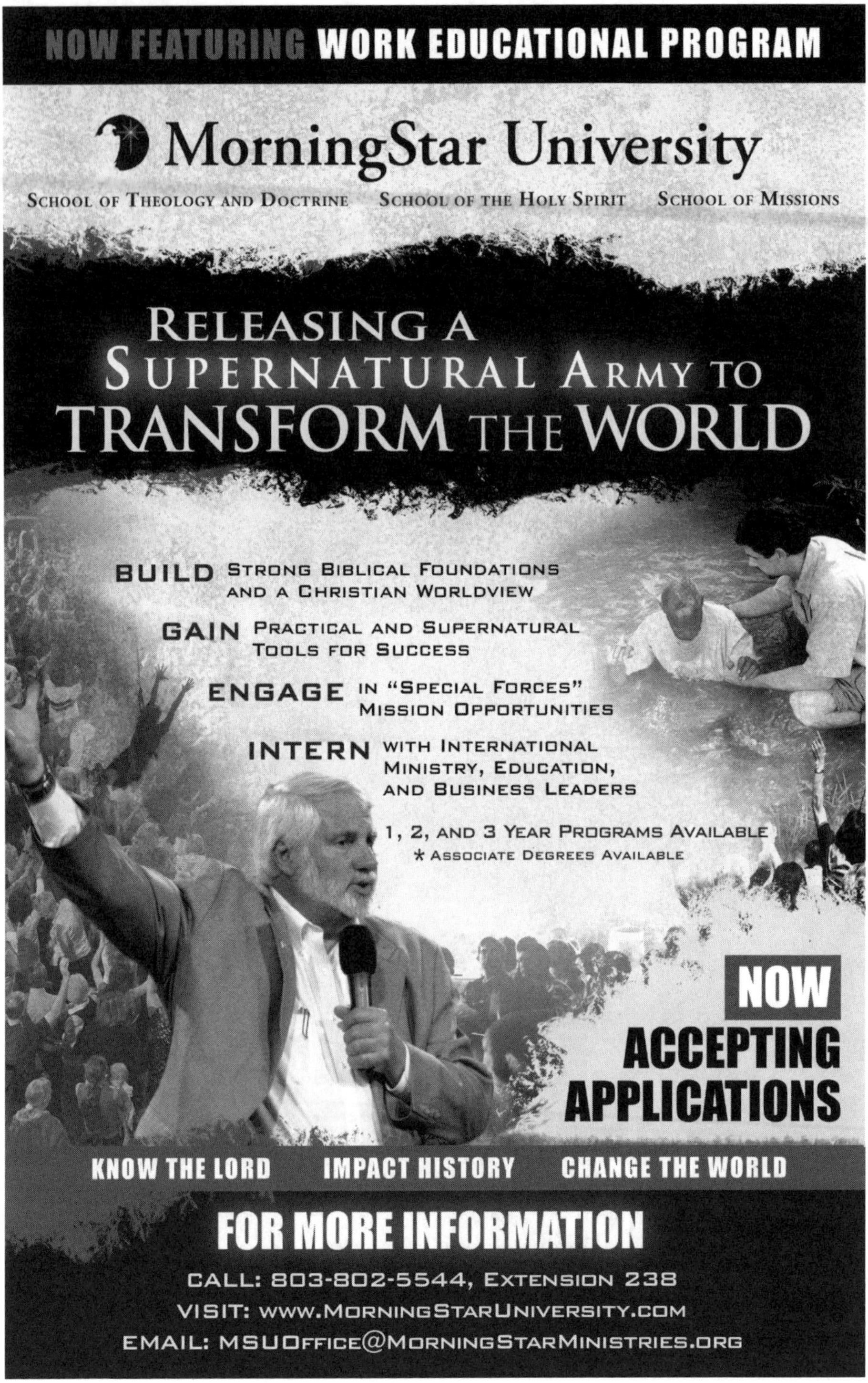
NOW FEATURING WORK EDUCATIONAL PROGRAM
MorningStar University
SCHOOL OF THEOLOGY AND DOCTRINE
SCHOOL OF THE HOLY SPIRIT
SCHOOL OF MISSIONS
RELEASING A SUPERNATURAL ARMY TO TRANSFORM THE WORLD
BUILD STRONG BIBLICAL FOUNDATIONS AND A CHRISTIAN WORLDVIEW
GAIN PRACTICAL AND SUPERNATURAL TOOLS FOR SUCCESS
ENGAGE IN "SPECIAL FORCES" MISSION OPPORTUNITIES
INTERN WITH INTERNATIONAL MINISTRY, EDUCATION, AND BUSINESS LEADERS
1, 2, AND 3 YEAR PROGRAMS AVAILABLE
* ASSOCIATE DEGREES AVAILABLE
NOW ACCEPTING APPLICATIONS
KNOW THE LORD
IMPACT HISTORY
CHANGE THE WORLD
FOR MORE INFORMATION
CALL: 803-802-5544, EXTENSION 238
VISIT: WWW.MORNINGSTARUNIVERSITY.COM
EMAIL: MSUOFFICE@MORNINGSTARMINISTRIES.ORG

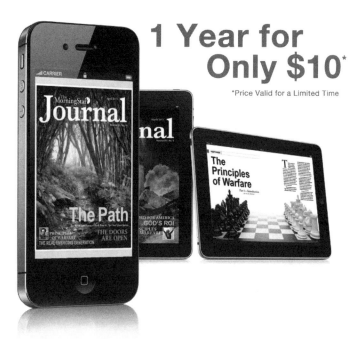